MIKE O'NEILL

DON'T
BACK
DOWN

Don't Back Down
By Mike O'Neill

The events and conversations in this book have been set down
to the best of the author's ability, although some names have
been changed to protect the privacy of individuals.

ISBN
Hardcover: 979-8-9873553-0-5
Paperback: 979-8-9873553-1-2
Ebook: 979-8-9873553-2-9
First edition 2023

Edited by Sarah Fox "The Bookish Fox"
Cover design by Damon Freeman "Damonza"
Layout by Damon Freeman "Damonza"
Photographs by Keith Renard, Roger Cotton, Ron O'Neill, Shaye Whiteman
Ebook design by Damon Freeman "Damonza"

coachmikeoneill@hotmail.com
Instagram@coachmikeoneill

INTRODUCTION

February 2020
Houston, Texas
8:30 a.m.

A S I ARRIVED at the entrance of MD Anderson Cancer Center that mild winter morning, my schedule was tight and my stay brief. I simply wanted to get these mandatory appointments behind me.

"Mr. O'Neill, I'll pick you up at 3:30 for your return flight to Bush International," said my driver.

"Thanks, Riaz, see you then," I replied.

My trip was to be very quick, hours to be precise. The purpose: to obtain head, neck, and chest scans, receive good news from my doctor I'm still cancer-free, and get back to my busy life in Tennessee.

Not the case.

"Mike, I have some bad news: Your cancer has potentially metastasized to the upper lobe of your right lung," my oncologist indicated.

Wait, no, this cannot be happening, not again.

This was the second time since 2017 I had received excruciating news about cancer becoming a part of my life. This time the prognosis was far more dire. Over the past two years, with the help of a great team, I had achieved the goal of remission through an intense treatment regimen that I hoped would cause the cancer to remain dormant for years to come.

The first diagnosis tested every fiber in my body; however, it provided a break in the clouds. My wife and I were able to take a sabbatical from "life in the fast lane" and appreciate what a wonderful marriage and family life had offered us.

Roughly one month after my second diagnosis, as COVID-19 reared its ugly head, I went back to Texas for lung surgery to extract my small tumor using a wedge technique. Unfortunately, it was confirmed that the nodule was squamous cell carcinoma that had metastasized from my throat. Furthermore, five more lesions were detected in both lungs. The news was beyond devastating.

What now?

As Beth and I made our way back to Memphis, I was delirious with concern. The school system in which I was employed made the decision to officially close due to the community spread of COVID-19. I was forced to teach remotely during the last quarter of the spring semester.

In short, I was now stage-four once again, only this time with no known cure during a global pandemic while being highly advised by my doctors to shelter in place for the foreseeable future.

While the days melted into one another, I began to ponder about my existence: What did all of this truly mean? My thoughts were shadowed by two questions: How much time do I have left, and what has my life meant until this very moment?

As Beth and I went through every possible scenario of my condition, I began to recollect and document my thoughts. Ultimately, I wanted to share my story with my family and generations beyond to help illustrate my time in this world and how I approached it.

By going back in time, I was able to slow down and examine my conscience and connect life events that have impacted and guided the most significant meaning to my sheer being. On the peripheral, I never experienced a huge amount of regret about how my life had played out, however, I was able to analyze my imperfections and struggle throughout my journey. As I recollected these events, I reevaluated my thought process and motivations that had led me to pursue my lifelong ambition of mentoring young people, finding my soulmate in the process, and raising three wonderful children.

My story is about how faith, love, and determination play such an important role in seeking life's most incredible gifts.

This book is an example of pursuing your true passion, while keeping an open mind to the possibilities and opportunities, and not being discouraged by unanticipated adversity that you will more than likely encounter along the way. This story chronicles my struggle both professionally and personally, and how it shaped my thinking about various decisions I made that ultimately impacted my life, both good and bad.

My story is chronological in nature and not focused on my cancer journey per se; to the contrary, my message is about a myriad of life lessons that prompted me to seek life's true calling and happiness while maintaining balance and meaning in my personal life. This narrative is certainly not a "how-to manual" but simply an account of someone going after their dream with the help of an incredible soulmate and not backing down in the process.

We never truly know how much time we have left. It just gratifies me to have the opportunity to explore the great queries of life and scrutinize how my journey has played out until this point.

This is my story...

CHAPTER 1

ONE DECISION, MAJOR CONSEQUENCES

I T WAS A long and extremely hot summer going into my junior year at Germantown High School in 1982. I was playing competitive baseball for the Term City Memphis Tigers baseball team. That summer was no different from most summers. When I was eleven, I began playing summer league baseball for the East Memphis Tiger Organization. Each season, they would hold tryouts in the spring, then play games almost every day of the summer. I started out playing fifty to sixty games as an eleven-year old, and by the time I was sixteen, we would play between seventy to eighty games in a single summer.

The season would consist of league and non-league games during the week and tournaments on the weekends. Around the end of July, we would start the postseason. Every year, our goal was to make it to the World Series. Back in those days, you had to earn your way there. Our league was the American Amateur Baseball Conference (AABC).

As I was getting older, the number of games we played increased.

The summer baseball season was lasting longer, school was starting earlier, and two-a-day football practices were pushed up a week to accommodate the earlier start to the school year. Simply put, baseball would transition into football season immediately.

So, in the summer of 1982, I was at a crossroad. I had just come off playing an eighty-game schedule, serving as the team's catcher for seventy of them. Along with baseball in the afternoon and evenings, I dug dig ditches for Ekmark Electric from seven a.m. until three p.m. That summer, I lost twenty-five pounds leading up to the two-a-day football practices. As the regional baseball tournament began, so did football. The tournament dragged out due to rain delays, and I entertained the idea of not playing football that season, possibly hanging up my cleats for good. In my mind, I knew that baseball was my ticket to a college scholarship, and I was tired and frustrated. Not only did I lose twenty-five pounds, but I was not growing.

I hadn't grown an inch since I was in seventh grade. I was one of those kids that reached puberty extremely early and could almost grow a full beard in middle school at five foot eight and 165 pounds. At the end of that summer in 1982, I was five foot eight and 155 pounds soaking wet. Being that size, I was kind of frustrated because I was an offensive lineman and an inside linebacker on defense. Because I always exceeded the weight limit to run the football every season in youth ball, every year I played in the trenches as a lineman. You name it, I played it—guard, tackle, and center on offense—however, my first love was inside linebacker on the defensive side of the ball because I could use my athleticism to make more plays. My favorite part of football was making those individual collisions.

During spring football practice in February earlier that year, I could tell my lack of size would hamper my ability as an offensive lineman. Also, missing a week of two-a-days with the extended baseball season sealed the deal. I made up my mind to hang the helmet up. Undoubtedly, it was a selfish thing to do. I should have approached Germantown's head football coach, Ken Netherland, long before a week after football had started and filled him in on my concerns. Being a head football coach later in life certainly helped me understand this, but I didn't get it when I was sixteen.

After we were eliminated from the regional baseball tournament at Gagliano Park on a hot August afternoon, mom, dad, and I made our way to the parking lot. As I opened the sliding door to the family van, I was overcome with anticipation about how this next conversation would unfold with them, mainly with my dad.

"Dad, Mom, I have been thinking over the past few weeks, and I have made a decision not to play football this season."

My dad Ron, rarely at a loss for words, sat in the driver's seat staring at me in the rearview mirror. He then repositioned his body to me in the back and spoke, "Mike, I think this is something you will regret moving forward."

Mom just sat there. She appeared to be somewhat relieved because she wasn't particularly a fan of me playing football to begin with.

He continued, "I know and understand how tough it is to play two sports at this level, but I think you will kick yourself over time. I know you're frustrated by not growing, but the coaching staff will help you make a transition to other positions that you are more suitable given your size and athletic ability."

"I have made up my mind, Dad. Baseball is my ticket. I need to focus on that completely. I have been thinking about this since spring practice, and my mind is made up."

Dad shook his head in disgust and made a last-ditch effort, reminding me of one of his high school classmates back in the late '50s.

"Tim McCarver, my old classmate at Christian Brothers, did both. Went on to play professional baseball in four decades and always said his favorite sport was high school football. You're going to regret this. Trust me!"

Dad could sense that I had already played this out in my mind and tapered the sales pitch back. "Okay, before you make it official, go tell Coach Netherland in person. This is non-negotiable!"

"Yes, sir," I said as my eyes made it back to the blue shag carpet floorboard.

Time to face the music. What do you say to the coach who eventually will be the second winningest high school head football coach in the state of Tennessee with 368 career victories? In 1982, he was on his way to making that happen. He'd had some tough years back in the mid-70s but started turning things around by the end of the decade. By 1980, he led Germantown to its first state championship game and won his first title in 1983.

I was a bit intimidated and nervous to fulfill that task, but thought there was no better time than the present. As the crow flies, I lived about three miles from his house in Germantown. I knew I probably would catch him in-between practices to make my case. Incidentally, that was the longest car ride I have ever experienced. The entire time, I was planning in my mind what I needed to say with the strong possibility of receiving a good old-fashioned butt-chewing because of my tardy announcement.

As I pulled up in front of his house, I saw his truck in the driveway. Time to get this over with. The dread was mounting, and I had no idea what to expect. While my heart was beating like I just ran the 200-meter hurdle, I saw Mrs. Netherland through the front-door window. She opened the door.

"Hi, Mrs. Netherland. My name is Mike O'Neill. I apologize for coming over unannounced, but would it be okay if I spoke with coach for a couple of minutes?"

"Not a problem," she politely replied. "Just give me a couple of minutes to get him from the backyard. Hold on."

What seemed like an eternity was only a couple minutes. My guess was he was finishing off one of those unfiltered Pall Mall cigarettes before he walked through the entry hall to meet me on the front porch.

"Mike O'Neill," he said in his distinct Yazoo City, Mississippi Southern drawl. "We missed you at practice this morning. Everything alright?"

I felt like an apple was at the base of my throat. I jumped right in. "Coach, I made the decision to concentrate on baseball moving forward. My prospects to play beyond high school are much better due to my size, and I cannot afford to break another bone heading into my junior year." After I finished stating my case, there was a brief pause.

"I would never try to talk someone into playing football if they were not fully committed to play, Mike." He continued, "I played college baseball at Ole Miss and understand the demands of a multiple-sports athlete and the commitment it requires. I will say the coaching staff were finding you another position that might better suit you on the football field, but it looks like you have made up your mind."

"Yes, sir. I'm sorry I didn't tell you sooner."

"Good luck with the baseball career," he said as he reached out to shake hands.

When I was walking to my car, I was grateful he did not guilt me, showed absolutely no anger, and did not attempt at all to talk me back into playing. As I stared at my Volkswagen Scirocco parked on the curb, I felt a sense of relief before I opened the door to return home.

A couple weeks passed, and I began having sports withdrawal. My plan was to play fall baseball, but that didn't start until mid-September. School still hadn't started, and all my time at Ekmark Electric was over for the summer. I honestly didn't know what to do or how to handle all that free time.

My parents gave me the green light to play any sport that I desired if I kept up my schoolwork. Funny, I look back now and appreciate what each sport contributed to my athletic ability overall. I was put on a soccer team at five years old because no other sports were offered at that age. At the time, soccer was quite established in the Dallas area. I played ten years of soccer, and the sport helped me with my overall footspeed and endurance. My football friends used to give me the business about soccer not being a contact sport, and I would remind them that I was the leading tackler on defense and could kick a football to the end zone on kickoffs. I probably had more injuries in soccer than any other sport I participated in over the years. Basketball was something for me to do to fill the gaps, but looking back, it helped me with my directional movement, which is critical when playing football.

Baseball came naturally due to my arm strength and because my football experience gave me the toughness to get behind the plate as a catcher, with all that gear on, in the brutally hot and humid Memphis summers. I liked catching because I was active every play, and I could see the whole field and sharpen my leadership skills in the process. Football and baseball really expanded my role as a leader, and almost every season, I was elected team captain for both sports. Football and baseball would lay the foundation for my eventual love of coaching.

As I became older, I had to make decisions about what to play and what not to play. I dropped basketball before high school. I played my last football/soccer combination season in the tenth grade. All those years I played soccer, they were for club teams. Varsity school soccer season was in the spring, and that wasn't going to happen because of the time constraints with baseball. Now that I had eliminated football, I was down to one sport—baseball!

The week before school started, my younger brother, Parks, went through the Germantown Youth Optimist Football Draft. To kill some time, because I had an ample amount of it now, I tagged along to see how my little brother would match up with the other kids. The next day, my parents received a phone call from Larry Watts to inform them that Parks would join his team for this football season. Larry then asked my dad if he could speak to me. To my complete surprise, my dad handed me the phone with Mr. Watts on the line. I already knew Mr. Watts because he was the father of one of my buddies, Elliot, who was a starting linebacker on the varsity football team. As my dad handed me the phone, I whispered, "Why does Mr. Watts want to talk to me?"

"Haven't the faintest," he said.

"Hey, Mike. Larry Watts here. Elliot told me you weren't playing ball this year. Do you have any interest helping me coach the junior division football team that Parks is a part of?"

He was downright insistent on me helping. Without any objections, I told him I would do it. I enjoyed the idea of staying busy and working with my kid brother while I had free time. I was not sure if Parks would enjoy it, but he didn't have any say in it. Practices would start around five thirty in the afternoon and wouldn't interfere with fall baseball practice. Mr. Watts said I could run the offense and install the wishbone and the five-two monster defense that Germantown High School had been running for some time. I had playbooks from last season, and most of it was fresh for me. My parents were excited I would be working with Parks, and this was a productive way to spend my free time.

As the preseason began, I was completely enthralled with installing play schemes on both sides of the ball and teaching the other coaches and players my knowledge of football. What I wasn't sure of, I would retrieve out of my detailed playbook provided by Coach Netherland and Jerry Ellis, the freshman coach. As the season began, I loved watching the players develop and get excited for the upcoming Saturday morning games. We didn't study film in that league but would scout other opponents during the times we weren't scheduled to play and look at other teams for information about personnel and schemes, so we could have productive practices leading up to game time.

As a player, it was hard to understand why coaches set up different drills and why they were so insistent on players being so precise to complete each task. I remember a defensive pursuit drill that required complete hustle and focus to accomplish it successfully. The problem was getting eleven guys to match the required intensity demanded from that coach. In order to make that happen, the drill started from the beginning again until *everyone* was on the same page. Why was everyone getting punished if one guy didn't fulfill his obligation? Now that I was on the other side, I really began to appreciate why the coaches went to this length. I understood you're only as good as your weakest link.

"Line up, guys. I need eleven players to the ball! Snap to whistle! No exceptions. Gentlemen, we are trying to develop discipline and promote accountability," I demanded.

It was starting to click. As time went on, I began to see another side of football and why players had to be all-in to be successful. I saw the big picture preparation and drill work were required to improve techniques. I was introduced to the psychological aspects of what motivated players. I understood what worked for some and what didn't work for others. Some kids were motivated by fear, while others were motivated by positive reinforcement. The process fascinated me, and over time, I figured out I would simply coach how I liked to be coached.

As a player, I liked that balance of discipline, but I enjoyed receiving praise when performing and giving great effort. Phrases like "snap to whistle" or "play like your hair is on fire" always got me going.

As the varsity football season concluded, I began to envision the possibility of playing football my senior year. I started to see football from another angle and was convinced I could make the transition to play other positions. My foot and directional speed were excellent, and my forty time was above average. Basically, I ran well for a former interior lineman and realized I could make a case to find a starting position on one side of the ball if I put my mind to it. Specifically on defense. Also, I didn't enjoy watching Friday night games from the stands. It just didn't feel right. I wouldn't let anyone in on my secret desire at this time, including my dad.

As Christmas came and went, the baseball preseason was in full force, and we were gearing up for a great year. Two years prior, I was a freshman letterman on the 1981 State Baseball Championship team at Germantown. Furthermore, baseball and basketball in West Tennessee were more of a presence overall compared to West Tennessee football, except for one school: Germantown.

CHAPTER 2

DAMN, NEILL!

THAT WINTER, SPRING football practice was over before baseball started; however, I decided to not to participate. I didn't want football to derail my plans for a great season or snap a wrist and be injured for an all-important junior campaign. I truly wanted to get through the school and summer baseball season to build my resume as the top catcher in the state. Even though I was leaning toward making a comeback in football my senior year, I gave baseball my complete attention. Also, during the several months between football seasons, I never told a soul about my ambition to play.

As the baseball tournament ended abruptly that late July Sunday afternoon, Dad asked me for the first time in about a year, "Are you playing football this fall?"

"I will be at the field house at 6:00 a.m. sharp to ask Coach Netherland in person if I can join the team this fall," I responded without hesitation as a huge smile appeared across my dad's face.

There was a good chance that coach would veto my plan because I blew off spring practice back in February and didn't participate in one football weight session offered over the summer. I knew the deck was stacked against me and that Coach Netherland rewarded preparation. Leaving his program usually meant that person couldn't rejoin the team. However, in my seventeen-year-old mind, I had a plan. My plan was to bust my ass during every single drill, every single play, every single practice.

At 6:00 a.m. on that hot August Monday, I was at the field house. It was already eighty-five degrees at 90 percent humidity. As I pulled up, just as I anticipated, I saw coach's truck parked in front of the field house. I knew he would be prepping for a long two-a-day practice to begin the 1983 football campaign. The main field house door was unlocked. I figured he would be in the coach's office, just left of the entrance. As I walked toward the office, there was a quick flashback of the sophomore head-shaving incident that happened two years prior. I quickly shoved that thought aside. I took a deep breath and gently knocked on the closed door.

"Come in!"

As I opened the door, our eyes met.

"Good morning, Mike O'Neill. Are you lost?"

"Good morning, coach. No, sir, I wanted to talk to you before practice to see if I could play football this season."

Before he could answer, I continued, "Coach, my plan is to bust my ass every second I'm on your field. I understand it would take a monumental effort on my part to get back on the team to contribute, not to mention a starting role somewhere on the field."

As I took another breath, he kept listening. "I realize that I haven't earned any senior privileges and would be thrilled to locker with the sophomores in the back of the locker room."

Basically, it was a self-imposed penance with the hope of making this an easy decision for Coach Netherland to make. What did I have to lose?

"You have a former player that could contribute and provide depth on both sides of the ball. Also, my leg strength could provide some value and contribute on special teams."

After my sales pitch, there was another long pause.

"The only reason I am agreeing to this is because you were man enough to come tell me in person that you were quitting the team last season," he said as he rose out from behind the desk to shake hands. "Welcome back! Coach Smith will be here in fifteen minutes and will pull your equipment. Tell him you have been assigned number thirty-four. You will report with defensive backs and fullbacks during individual periods. I will also grant your wish of being with the sophomores."

I was excited and relieved at the same time. "Thanks, Coach!"

He attempted a smile, nodded his head, and told me to shut the door.

"Yes, sir!"

As I was sitting in the back of the locker room with my newly issued football gear, other players started to show up for the 7:30 a.m. full-pad practice. Back in those days, there was no "heat acclimation period" to the beginning of August football camp that required players to practice in helmets for a few sessions before gradually allowing players into full gear to prevent heat exhaustion.

"Look, O'Neill's back," came a loud voice from the entrance of the locker room.

I could hear undertones of being a baseball-only guy.

"He didn't come to spring practice," bellowed a senior offensive lineman.

"I didn't see him in the weight room any this summer," chirped another kid.

I had certainly created a buzz on that hot August morning.

"Aren't you a senior?" one of the tenth graders asked in a smart-ass fashion as I sat in the middle of the sophomore section of the now cramped locker room. I didn't respond. My plan was to keep blinders on and limit distractions if it continued. I had several months to think about how that would play out. If I sat there and listened to the chatter and negative talk, I might have been consumed by it.

That first day, my only goal was to pick out the team's top hitter and lock horns. Howard Moss, a future All-SEC strong safety at Ole Miss, who had a reputation of being a massive headhunter, was that guy. I remember back in middle school, most players would avoid two guys in Oklahoma drills: Moss and O'Neill. The two starting inside linebackers. Now Howard was six foot two and weighed 190 pounds. He was a Division I SEC recruit.

After warmups, the schedule I read on coach's office chalkboard was true to form. Oklahoma time! There are different combinations you could use in the drill, but Germantown used a two-on-two technique with a running back to tackle to complete the drill. This drill was designed by Oklahoma Sooner's coach, Bud Wilkinson, to simulate full contact and was used by the NFL for years. Incidentally, the NFL has now discouraged this drill to prevent injury.

As blocking bags were put down by assistant coaches to set the perimeter of the drill, the tension mounted. I made sure I was in the opposing line to Moss. Funny, some guys will pick out the headhunters and make damn sure they are in the same line as them to avoid contact. Not me.

As the coaches set up the drill, I had pushed my way up to the top of the line, so I was facing Howard Moss. I remember pushing my way forward; other guys were relieved that I was taking their spot in line.

I was in a two-point stance across from an offensive guard that had about a three-foot split between him and the center. Moss was in the backfield with the football in hand. The moment Coach Smith blew the whistle, I shot through the gap untouched and hit Moss with a full head of steam about a yard behind the line of scrimmage. I timed it perfectly. Some guys told me later that it sounded like a shotgun went off. Everyone went wild, including Coach Leland Smith. Smith was one of those fire-and-brimstone coaches who never held back any emotion. After I hit Moss with an incredible blow, Smith picked me up by the shoulder pads and yelled in my face, "Number thirty-four came to play. Moss and O'Neill, line up again."

Now at this point, the other three guys were not invited back. It was just me and Moss about seven yards away. Oklahoma drill quickly went to a Bull in the Ring matchup. Only two players line up to make a collision. Moss and I were about to make a second one inside of thirty seconds of this practice period. Coach Smith said, "Ready," blew the whistle, and we met like two battering rams! We both fell to the ground almost simultaneously next to one another. From the moment of contact, I saw stars, and by the look on Howard's face, he saw the same.

"Damn, Neill!" was the only thing he said.

From that point on, I knew I could play not only with anyone on the team, but I was not going to be intimidated by anyone in the state! Now to impress the rest of the coaching staff.

CHAPTER 3

RELENTLESS AS USUAL

AS FOOTBALL CAMP went into week two, I continued my onslaught of making collisions and gaining praise from the staff. Football camp was essentially to determine where aggression was and seek out hitters. Every hitting drill, I would attempt to target other impact players. Chris Coppedge, another top running back, was one of my best friends and summer baseball cohort. Chris was an All-Metro halfback and, at the age of eleven, had a nice write-up in the *Germantown News* about his future prospects as a running back after he gained 2,500 yards on an eighty-yard field as a fifth grader. Running him down back in those days was next to impossible.

During team practice, I flat-out insisted to Coach Charlie White, my defensive back coach, that I could play on the scout defense with the other sophomores while I waited for my reps as a backup on offense.

As the defensive huddle broke, Coach White instructed, "Thirty-four! Blitz B-Gap this rep." The play was called and the timing was perfect. I lit Chris up on an off-tackle belly play, and he didn't see me coming. As Chris and I got off the ground, he said, "Okay, O'Neill. I see how it is."

In Chris's defense, he wasn't expecting someone on the scout team to go full contact. In my mind, there was not a set of rules for this drill session, and this felt like a fantastic situation to show my worth and ability.

I was the only senior (along with ten sophomores) on scout team that fall camp, creating an uncomfortable situation for starters by requiring them to increase their effort and awareness every single play; I wore that as a badge of honor. Before I knew it, eleven scout team All-Americans were hammering the first team on offense, and it was pissing people off. The practice team was bringing their A game, and the coaches loved it. Especially the defensive coaches. Coach Smith, who was enthusiastic and extremely boisterous, was bouncing around picking defensive scout team players up from the pile, getting in their faces to let them know their effort was appreciated.

"Nice effort! Look at those starters getting yelled at! Keep it up!" he would often remind us.

When special team period began, I lined up one day on the perimeter defending the field goal unit. With a hand in the dirt and a sprinter's stance, I figured out the rhythm of the snap count and I was a half-step from anyone being able to block me. That practice, I blocked multiple kicks by laying out and getting a piece of the ball, changing the trajectory of flight. I knew when special team coaches were tearing into their guys from a lack of concentration or not completing the assignment; my plan of creating disruption continued to work. I began to hear guys on the point after attempt team say, "Watch out for O'Neill."

"O'Neill is lined up here."

"Dammit, O'Neill! What the hell is your problem?"

I would just laugh. Sometimes I replied, "Your lack of effort is the damn problem."

I will add that our field goal team was perfect that season. The kinks were worked out in camp, and I won the job as the edge blocker on the field goal team in the process.

My plan of drawing attention to my relentless effort began to pay off. After two weeks of camp, the coaching staff chose the players they wanted to be a part of their special teams. Coach Netherland had a system where each position coach was responsible for an individual special team. On paper, Coach Netherland oversaw all the teams, but assistant coaches were responsible for the execution and the overall success of the team they managed. The staff had the freedom to choose any player who they felt would give it their all and who would not take any plays off because they played on offense or defense. Everyone was available for every special team, no matter who played where. So, as a result, each coach would not hold back at all.

That special teams practiced while we stood on the sidelines to the game field, I anticipated that my hard work was about to pay off. Each position coach would call out player names and positions of his special team.

"O'Neill, line up!"

"O'Neill, get over here!"

On every single special team, my name or number was picked either first or second every time. In addition to my work in the kicking game, I played on the short yardage goal line package that was executed by the offense inside the red zone at the plus seven-yard line and beyond.

Along with successful special team play and short yardage offensive package, I found myself in a backup role at strong safety and provided depth as a backup fullback. I wanted more. As the season opened, my work ethic and attitude continued to thrive. I never became frustrated; however, I wanted more than special teams, goal line packages, and clean-up duty at the end of games. As once a two-way starter, it was in my blood to become a starter once again.

By week five, I was doing my regular routine of making excellent contributions on special teams and providing running lanes on goal line offense while getting some garbage time as a backup if the games were blowouts. However, the three games were dog fights, and we lost our homecoming game to the eventual Arkansas state runner-up, Pine Bluff, late in the game while scratching out a narrow victory over a motivated Bartlett team to win our first district game. So, now we were 3-1, and the past three games were a complete struggle. Unfortunately, during the close win against Memphis University School two weeks prior, Mark Bowen, a future Memphis State signee, tore his ACL at his inside linebacker position and was out the rest of the season. During the Bartlett game, the inside linebacking core rotated backups to attempt to put together a successful performance. It clearly didn't happen during that contest, and we were absolutely gashed through A/B gaps all night. With Bowen injured, that left a sizeable gap in our defense.

The following week, we traveled to Millington Tennessee to take on another average Millington Trojan squad. Now, the staff started to give Moss reps at inside linebacker and provided more reps for me at strong safety during practice that week. This was the opportunity I had been waiting for. Two things were paramount during Millington practice week: 1) continue to bust my ass and keep a great attitude on the practice field, and 2) keep my dad in check! He was livid at my playing situation. He not only thought, but was convinced, that I needed to be on the field somewhere, somehow. He felt that way going into the Bartlett game. By Wednesday of that week, Dad was ready to make a visit to the field house on my behalf. That's when we had a man-to-man conversation.

That Monday after practice I pulled in the driveway, and Dad was waiting out front. Tired and hungry, I began the conversation as I exited my car, "What's up, Dad?"

"Mike, get back in the car," he said as he grabbed my passenger door handle.

"Where are we going?" I asked because I hadn't the faintest idea about what he was thinking.

"I'll tell you on the way to the practice field. Are Netherland and Smith still up there?"

"I am sure they are, but we are *not* going up there! Dad, stay out of it! I understand the frustration, believe me, but you putting pressure on the staff will not help. I will get on the field on my own merit. Trust the process. I will find a way to make an impact."

My mom, dad, and the whole family were in on the conversation, and it was a knock-down-drag-out on Cornwall Street that evening.

"Please, Dad. Stay out of it!"

Somehow, I talked my dad out of taking that unscheduled journey to the field house, but he stated he wouldn't make any future promises if I continued to get screwed out of playing time.

That Friday, we played Millington on the road and fell behind two touchdowns before halftime. The defensive game plan was clearly not working. During the first and second quarters, backup linebackers played in rotation much like the Bartlett game, and the results were similar. Clearly, the Millington coaching staff did an excellent job of exploiting the deficiencies of the inside linebacker. At halftime, I remembered Coach Smith and Coach White met in a closed-door office of the visitor locker room before the defense was invited up. I kept thinking, *Stay alert! Stay focused, and be ready for anything. Above all, do your job.*

Coach Smith, our defensive coordinator, gave some simple yet loud instructions as he slammed the office door behind him, storming out. "Shut the hell up and get your heads out of your ass!"

He was on fire as he marched into the cramped corner where the unit was gathered. By this time, he was pacing back and forth between some lockers and a small chalkboard. As he continued for a couple more passes, he made it back to the blackboard, picked up the small box of unopened chalk that our managers had packed for the road trip and promptly threw them clear across the locker room where it shattered into pieces on the opposite wall. Nobody said a word as we watched in horror. He clearly had seen enough for two quarters, and plan B was now about to be implemented. He was raging.

"Moss! Get your ass to Will linebacker. O'Neill, get your ass to strong safety! We will line up in Cover Three Diamond to start the third quarter." Cover Three Diamond in our five-to-two monster defense meant adjusting the strong safety line up two yards in depth behind the inside linebackers directly over the center. I would have run responsibility first and was instructed to move to the football immediately to slow down the penetration coming through A and B gaps.

Coach Smith continued, "When we stuff that, we will get back into Cover Three. O'Neill, you will adjust to the tight end side and might bring you off the edge with Flex-Ex on certain downs."

"Yes, sir!" I replied with authority. At that moment, I would have run through a brick wall had he asked. We had been practicing for this very plan-B scenario in team period this week.

We began the second half on defense. I was locked and loaded. My focus was steady, and my nerves were surprisingly in check. As we broke the huddle, I began my first duty as the strong safety.

"Strong left! Strong left! Cover Three Diamond!" I yelled as loud as I possibly could.

While standing over the center about five yards deep, I watched the rest of the offensive linemen walk up to get their two-yard splits. As the quarterback approached the line of scrimmage, he checked the remainder of the players to ensure they were lined up properly before he started the cadence. My heart raced.

As pre-snap turned into the play, my only read was the fullback. I had to go meet him at the line of scrimmage or the backfield. I must blow up the block or make the tackle. In the first half, he had close to ten carries alone.

The QB took the snap, opened to his right, and put the ball into the gut of their stocky fullback. Just about the moment he took the handoff, my shoulder pads and Riddell helmet introduced him to a thunderous tackle about a yard deep in the backfield. Millington's game plan was clearly to stay the course.

On the second play, they ran off tackle on the other side, and I met the fullback at the line of scrimmage about as hard as I hit Moss on that practice during Oklahoma drill. Millington kept trying inside gaps, and Moss, Watts, and I were having a complete field day in Cover Three Diamond. For me, it was a defender's dream. I was completely unaccounted for and making huge hits every play on the ball carriers. The Cover Three Diamond formation was a brilliant adjustment because we hadn't shown it on film. Millington simply didn't have an answer for it.

As the defense ran to the sidelines after we stuffed them three series in a row, Coach Smith was in a much better mood. "Keep playing your ass off, defense, but let's be ready to adjust. They can't keep running this if we continue to stone them. Be ready!"

As we started back for the fourth series on defense, I felt a tug on my shoulder pad as I started to run on the field and stopped dead in my tracks.

"Thirty-four, you having fun yet? Go out there and keep having fun!" Coach Smith said with a big grin on his face as he turned to spit a solid five-inch stream of Redman on the Millington sideline.

"Yes, sir!"

As if Coach Smith had a crystal ball, the Trojans decided to test the perimeter of the strong side, and that's when we made our adjustment back to our Five-Two Monster. Flex-Ex was a blitz, where I simply traded responsibilities with the six technique (defensive end) and went through C-gap at full speed. I was at the point of attack almost every single play. I never saw the official stats from the game, but my dad said he recorded at least eleven tackles in that half and most of them were solo. We completely shut them down in the second half with zero points and maybe one first down. The offense, led by Coach Rocky Graves, went to another gear and made some adjustments in the passing game, which is extremely rare in our wishbone offense, but our talented QB, Forrest Nabors, and wideout, Bond Tubbs, connected for four passing touchdowns and won the game. Millington didn't know what hit them.

After the game, I knew I won the starting position at strong safety and our football team moving forward would be a force to be reckoned with. The ship was now pointed in the right direction.

CHAPTER 4

HOW DO YOU WANT TO BE REMEMBERED?

O WIN A state championship on any level is not an easy thing to do. My first taste of a high school state championship came my freshman year when GHS won the 1981 State Baseball AAA crown. Forrest Nabors and I were the only freshmen on that phenomenal team and we lettered in the process. As a competitive summer league baseball player, the tiger teams in which I played won five state titles; however, there was nothing like being crowned high school state champions. Heck, each player received a key to the city of Germantown.

The 1983 Germantown football team was about to change the direction of that narrative. In the beginning of camp, attitudes, hard work, and commitment were in great form. The season started out with two decisive victories against Booker T. Washington and West Memphis, Arkansas. We faced an excellent McMinnville team across the state and won in a defensive struggle.

However, this game exposed some issues during the overnight stay. A few players and members of the cheer squad broke curfew and were busted by the coaching staff making their rounds. Our archrival, Memphis University School, we beat in a close game at Germantown. MUS would end up having a fantastic year and lose in the AA State Championship game to Austin East. Homecoming was next, and we lost to a Pine Bluff Zebra team. After the next two narrow victories at Bartlett and Millington, some soul-searching was in order.

After Friday's come-from-behind victory, Coach Smith met with the defensive players, and his tone completely changed. His regular in-your-face, bouncing-around self was now laser focused. He started out by saying, "You have the rest of your lives to experiment with drugs, alcohol, and sneaking out past curfew on a high school football trip. Most of you will never play another down of organized football ever again after your senior year. For some of you seniors, your last days *in* any other organized sports will soon be over."

After a long pause and total silence, Coach Smith asked, "How do you want to be remembered? How does your senior class want to be remembered? You need to decide right here! Right now! How committed are you to this team? How committed are you to one another? This staff can sit here and yell at you all day long, but, ultimately, it must come from you! How committed are you? Not to be compared with some of the other Germantown teams that were not committed and downright selfish from the years past. This year is your year. We have the talent, support from the administration, an off-season program like no other, and community support demanding success in the immediate future. What is missing is your total commitment. Seniors, it starts with you. The rest will follow. You have the rest of your lives to try other stuff."

As Coach Smith walked out of the field house, you could have heard a pin drop. As the meeting adjourned, I felt like Coach Smith spoke directly from the heart. His message was crystal clear.

At that very moment, I noticed all the seniors who didn't play defense had made their way to our end of the field house. As we stood there, looking at one another, different seniors started to chime in.

"The partying stops right now," someone blurted out.

"Our commitment is shit; Coach Smith is right. It's time to refocus and get our crap together, that includes alcohol, weed, and anything else we don't need," a senior from the offensive side of the ball added.

"Yeah," another player said. "That goes for cigarettes, cigars, and getting wasted on the weekends too."

After about ten minutes of yelling and finger-pointing, a final decision was made, in effect immediately until the night of December 3, the date of the state championship game.

We all agreed and decided that a zero-tolerance policy on booze and drugs would be mandatory. This meeting was the most productive thing we did all season.

Along with the no-party rule, guys tried to get more sleep, hydrate, and eat better. At times, position coaches would have gatherings to enhance our discipline efforts by rewarding players with random food while discussing tactics or scheme. If you need to get the attention of a high school male, throw food in the mix. Furthermore, the football team's policy on negative behavior was spreading throughout the school in a good way. Fighting or embarrassing oneself on the weekend was not an option. The discipline and maturity of this squad began to evolve as the season unfolded.

CHAPTER 5

STATE CHAMPIONS OF THE WORLD

I WAS THRILLED MY first varsity start would come against our archrivals, -CBHS. The game started with a flash. On the first offensive play from scrimmage, Chris Coppedge parted the Red Sea and took it eighty yards with barely a minute in the contest. The beatdown continued, and the "Purple Wave" was taken to the woodshed that Friday night. During my first start, I collected twelve tackles, and two of them were for a loss. Looking back, everyone on our team had the attitude of "we will win!"

The game with Christian Brothers High School was the turning point of the season. As we moved forward in our schedule, we continued to destroy everyone in our path. As a result, we captured the District 14AAA Championship and qualified for the state football playoffs.

Four games had to be won to achieve our goal to capture the first ever Gold Ball in school history. After our last regular season post-game film session on Saturday, we decided as a program to take it one contest at a time. As a team, we made yet another commitment to one another and held each other accountable in playing in the present by maintaining complete focus to detail in every practice, film sessions, and walk-throughs we would have. Every sprint or drill would be embraced and enjoyed. Germantown was primed and ready for success.

Round one of the state playoff was against Lexington High School. Because we were the higher seed, we would host and play our last game on the Red Devil field. That week, the coaching staff did a great job of overhyping their All-State running back. The defense held him under fifty yards and a shutout while the offense lit up the scoreboard. Round one: Germantown 41 – Lexington 0.

Round two was against the top Memphis area team, Memphis Central. The game was played at Liberty Bowl Memorial Stadium in midtown Memphis. On a cool, clear Saturday night, the Red Devils took it to the Warriors in a one-sided victory. Round two: Germantown 35 – Memphis Central 8.

Round three was a road trip to Nashville to take on #1 seed undefeated Gallatin. Gallatin had only lost one game over the past two years and that went to the hands of Lincoln County 13 – 10, the prior December in the 1982 State Championship game. These guys were extremely motivated, and our coaching staff played that card like no other. As always, the staff on Sunday were over the top with a solid game plan. Along with dissecting the offensive-defensive scheme and how to attack each aspect of our opponent including a detailed depiction of special teams, the staff took it to another level.

Our coaching staff didn't admit this back then, but they felt like the state championship was round three in Gallatin, Tennessee. We were ready to take the field after we left the visitor's locker room after pregame warmups. As we marched up the hill in pairs to the north end zone, I noticed the visiting stands were now completely empty. They were empty because the Germantown faithful marched down to the field and built a human path between the goal line to the fifty. Students, fans, parents, and faculty formed this red path. My heart rate was off the chart. Our team was as hyped. After the conclusion of the national anthem, we sprinted to the sidelines! At around the thirty-five-yard line, I got blindsided by my dad before the first play. "Dammit, son! Let's kick their ass!"

One of the best collisions that night might have been between my father and me before the game even started. I learned later that Dad was on the parent/booster bus. Dad, who never met a stranger, directed everyone out of the visitor stands and orchestrated the massive tunnel, and the team fed off that energy.

The very first play, opening kickoff coverage, I made my presence known.

As I broke the wedge untouched, I got a shot on a ball carrier that hitters live for. It wasn't cheap or dirty, but it was totally clean. When the jarring impact was made, the ball was fumbled out of the returner's hands as I landed right on top of it. A few plays later, our wishbone offense made it to the visitor's end zone for the early lead. We never looked back.

Everything was close to perfection that Friday night. Final score: Germantown 31 – Gallatin 3.

State championship game week was like no other. As usual, our coaching staff was hard at work to produce another incredible game plan. It was announced late Friday after our game that our opponent for the Gold Ball would be the undefeated Jefferson County High School from East Tennessee.

I realized at the conclusion of the week that it would be my last for playing organized football. Coach Smith had drilled that in our heads. From time to time, he would remind us.

"One more week left before most of you turn into a week-end warrior!"

Basically, your days are numbered before you turn into a has-been.

As the practice week began, a sense of excitement was apparent, but I also felt at times sad. Personally, I didn't want this to end. Maybe because I took my junior year off and wanted more football.

As the week drew closer to the championship on Saturday,

many "lasts" were happening: the last full-pad practice, the last film session, the last Thursday night informal hangout, and the last two-hundred-yard timed sprint on the track. The week wrapped up with a walk-through at Red Devil field to tie up any loose ends for the final game. We had a meeting with Coach Smith and Coach White in the coach's office for the defense after that walk-through.

As he began to speak, Coach White started flipping out red bandannas with our individual numbers inscribed on them. Coach Smith spoke up as Coach White performed his task, "Bandannas were used by soldiers during the time of war to clean weapons and used for tourniquets after being wounded or simply wipe the brow of a dirty, sweaty forehead after a long battle."

The emotion began to seize that tiny office as tears began to trickle down the jawline of Smith's face. He continued without missing a beat. "I'm proud of each one of you. You know what the most powerful emotion is?"

No one answered.

"Love. Love is the most powerful emotion, and I love everyone in this room. Our bond will not be broken because we go to war. Play for the guy next to you."

As a defensive unit, we were completely astonished about what we had witnessed. Oh, hell yes, we were winning this football game!

CHAPTER 6

CLOSE THE DEAL

A S WE STOOD in the tunnel at Vanderbilt Stadium, ready to take the field after the AA game was deep in the fourth quarter, an intense rainstorm was on display. I heard a guy deep in the huddle under the overhang of the tunnel say, "It looks like an MTV music video."

About the time the game began, the all-day rain event came to a complete stop. The artificial turf was hard and slippery. Earlier that week, we practiced at Memphis State's indoor turf room, and they gave each player used turf shoes for the championship game at Vanderbilt. This was the old turf—basically a green rug on top of a concrete foundation. Eventually, teams would change this surface because of all the ACL injuries caused by this old turf. Personally, I had shin splints for two weeks after that final game.

The game started with a sensational kickoff return and a quick score by the Red Devil offense. Now it was time to play some defense. On the ensuing kickoff, I made a hard solo tackle, then made three more in the first defensive series. Before we got the ball back for our second drive, I had four tackles in the books. We jumped out to a fourteen-point lead and never looked back.

As the game proceeded, the defense continued to stifle the Patriot Wing T offense, and the tackles mounted. To my complete satisfaction, our scheme versus their wing T offense allowed me to remain unblocked most of the night while racking up tackles by the bunches.

It appeared pre-snap that we only had seven in the box because I was lined up roughly ten yards deep, equivalent with the free safety. However, on the snap, I had a pure run read, and I was coached to move downhill simultaneously as the play began to get back in the box quickly. I almost felt like they were running my way every time. Essentially, we were playing rotation coverage, and I was shooting down to the box every play, either making tackles or creating piles. Jefferson County never picked this up. I was unaccounted for the entire game. Germantown High School won their first football state championship in school history!

As I was taking off my game jersey and shoulder pads in the confines of the locker room, I understood this would be the last time ever I would perform this task in football. I realized more baseball was in my future. My football career was coming to a screeching halt as I walked off the field that December night. I was overcome with sadness and simply didn't want this to end.

I cried in my locker.

CHAPTER 7

FORKS IN THE ROAD – "THE COLLEGE YEARS"

MY ATHLETIC CAREER wasn't exactly panning out as I had projected. As I graduated high school in 1984, my original plan was to play Division I college baseball, study something in business, and then take a shot at professional ball at some point. It turned out my skills behind the plate continued to improve, and I built a reputation as one of the best defensive catchers in the region. I had a sense of pride every time I put on the gear to get behind the plate ever since grade school.

My junior year, I only had one runner all year steal a base, two passed balls, and no errors. My hitting was well above average, but my defense always outshined my batting average. During my junior school and summer season, I started to get noticed by several colleges for my skills. Not playing football my junior year to concentrate on baseball began to pay off. As I started to get recruited, my goal to play Division

I and beyond seemed to be going in the right direction. However, that summer, something started to go awry.

The spring and summer of 1984 were filled with tons of baseball. Day after day, night after night, doubleheaders, with infield, throwing between innings, the overuse was taking a major toll on the health of my arm.

While my shoulder started to deteriorate during the summer before college, so did my scholarship opportunities. Schools that originally were interested in a great defensive catcher with leadership ability and a batting average that improved in hitting over four hundred during my senior school campaign began to evaporate. I really started to feel the effects of my damaged arm with searing pain and discomfort that worsened as the summer rolled on. I refused to share what I was experiencing because I didn't want to be out of the lineup. However, as time went on, I was struggling to throw bases and eventually back to the pitcher. My lack of arm strength became obvious, which led to sitting out games, and college scouts began to realize I was injured.

Now, my damaged arm, along with my average grades and an ACT score that wasn't setting the world on fire, prevented some four-year schools to take a chance by offering a preferred walk-on opportunity, with the hope of a successful rehabilitation while taking a redshirt during my freshman year. Result, the only prospects moving forward were junior colleges. I was frustrated that my original plan was in jeopardy. I essentially put all my eggs in one baseball basket. At that time of my life, the thought of plan B never crossed my mind, not even once.

By August, I received an offer from Columbia State Community College in Columbia, Tennessee, about forty miles south of Nashville. I signed in late July. Upon arriving in Columbia, nothing guaranteed me playing immediately, or to have success in the classroom. CSCC had an incredible baseball history, and the competition was beyond fierce. After my freshman year, seven players were drafted in the major league June draft. The school was loaded with baseball talent. I quickly learned the goals of about half of the players on the roster were essentially to use junior college in order to get drafted after their freshman or sophomore season. At the four-year or university level, one had to play through their junior year to qualify for the draft back in the eighties. Two-year colleges did not follow those rules.

One thing was for certain, I didn't want to go the community college route to ride the oak. However, I knew there was massive work to do, but I knew I had to re-establish my arm strength before spring arrived. During that first week on campus, I had to take a placement exam to determine the level of English and math courses to take. I signed up to take fifteen hours for the first quarter.

On the diamond, I was in a heated battle with another kid from Illinois. During that fall, the staff developed a rehab program for my arm, which included rest by not playing fall baseball that year. During the layoff, I was able to manage my tendonitis that had severely affected my shoulder. A regimen of cortisone shots, rest, and specific exercises allowed my arm to heal until the start of preseason in January. By the first game in late February, I won the starting catcher position with five starts before the pain came back in my shoulder. I was back to injury status after three weeks. Frustrated but focused, I endured another rehab stint and eventually won the position back before the postseason started. That season we went on a successful postseason run but lost in the regionals.

Unbeknownst to me, my dad was doing some research on his own. He reached out to Jim Miles, the head coach at Northwest Junior College in Senatobia, Mississippi, to check out their catching needs. At that time, the Rangers graduated a sophomore and did not have a presence behind the plate and informed Dad they were familiar with me and welcomed the opportunity to work with me next season. With a week left of exams, Dad asked me if I was interested in playing for Northwest next season because they had a spot for me. I said, "Why not?" It was closer to home and would give me a new outlook. I packed up my gear, informed the staff at Columbia of my transfer, and headed West.

When I returned to Memphis, I was primed and ready for another summer of baseball. As always, our schedule was packed; however, I was able to rest my arm by rotating catching duties with the current Memphis State starting catcher. It turned out to be a great summer, and I formed many friendships in that two-month period. That fall, I started my tenure at Northwest in nearby Senatobia, Mississippi, about fifty miles south of Memphis.

When I arrived for my sophomore year, I was eager to see that we had a full fall baseball/practice schedule for that period. Jim Miles and Don Castle were the best baseball coaches that I ever played for. They both played for the Washington Senators and later for the Texas Rangers for a period. After their playing days, both decided to return to their home state where they began coaching college baseball together. Those guys were legendary and could have coached anywhere at any level. But I truly believe they both wanted to raise families in a small town, make a huge impact on young players, and fish to their hearts' content. Over time, many championships and world series appearances were accomplished. After twenty-plus seasons, Coach Miles retired and became athletic director, and Coach Castle took over the head job for the next ten years.

That fall after moving to Senatobia, I was enamored with both of their coaching styles. First, both men were extremely engaging and motivated in building personal relationships with each player that set foot on campus. Also, they set up an environment to be successful as an athlete and encouraged the baseball players to take accountability and achieve excellence in the classroom. Their leadership and coaching style appealed to me. They had very high standards and held players accountable for their actions.

My sophomore year at Northwest Junior College, I could tell I was mentally more mature and had a better respect for discipline. The foolish road trips and almost nightly parties began to dissipate from my Columbia State days. We still had fun at Northwest, but I figured out I needed to pick my battles. It was time to revisit the lessons

I learned from Leland Smith two short years prior during the state championship football run. *"You have the rest of your life to act like an idiot."* It's like the lightbulb was turned on once again, and Miles and Castle were the reason why.

Two important goals needed to be accomplished between then and late spring: 1) get academically eligible for a four-year university, and 2) win the job, play hard, and get recruited by a Division I program. Overall, I knew my goals that I set back in high school could still be accomplished. Only this time, academics played a major role in my planning.

That fall, my arm continued to heal, and I quickly won the catching job behind the plate. With Coach Castle's hitting instruction, I was making major improvement in that area also. Furthermore, I was going to take the leadership role to ensure the team had a great opportunity to get to the Junior College World Series played in Colorado in early June. Simply put, a trip to the World Series meant more opportunities to get exposure from every level of baseball.

Over the winter months, I dedicated myself to the strength program and began to see results. My work with Coach Castle in the indoor hitting facility in the basement of the Coliseum were paying dividends. Furthermore, on the academic front, hitting every class was the only option. Roll was taken for the baseball players and was reported if you blew it off. The curriculum was solid for my business major, and I finally felt balanced and challenged at the same time. Life was good.

When the spring season started, I knew we had an opportunity to be pretty good. I had played with or against most of the guys on the roster. We didn't have as much raw talent as Columbia State, but I felt like we had a good mix of pitching, defense, and hitters. We had some players with great speed on the base paths and we were solid up the middle defensively.

In taking over the leadership role, it was critical to evaluate talent; however, I quickly realized how important it was to determine personalities and what made guys tick. The one year of coaching during my junior year in high school helped me understand the important role of attitude and how people are motivated. One concern I had was that many guys on the team enjoyed having a good time. I personally went through that the previous year and knew it was time to take a page out of Coach Smith's playbook on this issue. I took it upon myself to call a team meeting, a week before the first series was to be played.

After I ran the idea by a couple teammates for feedback prior to the meeting, one informed me this would be next to impossible.

"College kids won't buy into this idea, these guys are away from their parents now, you'll see," explained Paul Bakke, whom I had played summer ball with since first grade.

Never, however, did I feel like my plan wouldn't work. I knew at Germantown High School, the '83 football team had some major partiers, and we bought into an alcohol-free season. If I could sell them on this "no-party clause" and get on them board, we would have major success in the process. Getting to and winning the World Series was the goal.

One Sunday night, after a preseason practice, I planned time in the lobby of the athletic dorm for a team meeting. To my surprise, every single player showed up. As players gathered in the dorm conference room and found a seat, the questions started.

"What's up?" came a voice from the back of the room.

"What's the meeting about? Someone in trouble?" came from the same direction.

After everyone was accounted for, I began the meeting. I could see the looks of confusion as I started my message. Some of them were starting to fidget while some stood with folded arms. A couple guys were shaking their heads in disgust because of this unofficial team meeting called by the new guy, who just showed up only one semester prior. Quickly, I was getting a negative vibe and losing the room. *I better get this thing started pronto*, I thought.

"In short, show me by raising your hand if you want to play beyond your days at Northwest at a four-year college or the professional level?"

As the question was posed, every hand went up.

"Good." Now the eye contact started to increase.

"I didn't drag you down here to waste your time tonight, but I think it's important I share with you a thought I had a couple of nights ago. I believe *everyone* sitting in this room just agreed they would like to extend their baseball careers beyond this season, correct?" Some nodded in agreement. "Now the question is: how do we get there?

"The further we go, the more exposure everyone will have. There will be more colleges and pro scouts the longer we stay alive. If we are still playing in June, the sky is the limit."

The message was straightforward; however, it was like an epiphany to many sitting in that dorm meeting room.

"It's simple. Our best road to accomplish this goal is to win every conference series in the regular season and we host the Mississippi Junior College State Baseball Tournament. Our chances double if we host—no bus rides, no hard hotel beds, and fast food. We win State; we have a one series playoff in the region with the Louisiana champion to see who goes to the World Series in Grand Junction, Colorado." The body language now contained nods of approval and demanded a response check. "Is this something you're interested in?"

"Hell yeah," came a voice from the back of the room after five or so seconds of silence after my last question.

"Here's the deal. *Everyone* in this room *must* buy in to make this thing work! Everyone. No exception."

After the lofty goal was set, I went with yet another question: "How committed are you to get this done? We can say we want this. We say we will do this, but how much skin do we put into this to increase our chances of hitting our goals? How committed are you?"

Nothing was said, but I had everyone's attention. I went on to say, "This spring, let's maximize our efforts and commitment for Ranger baseball."

Some guys were still looking at one another and some of them weren't exactly sure where I was going.

"Most of you guys are familiar with the Germantown football program that won state two years ago?"

Most were nodding their heads because it received major press. Most of them remembered it as one of the biggest high school sports stories in years.

"The key to that year wasn't the wealth of talent we had; it was the commitment to win by eliminating the distraction of drugs and alcohol during the season." I told them the story about Coach Smith's speech to the senior players that day at Germantown.

"If it's not good for the team, don't do it. Get your rest, stay out of trouble, and no fighting." As my message was sent, I could see that they were buying what I was selling. I'm not quite sure if all the guys followed suit, but probably most of them did. I told them if we could start the season with this attitude and commitment, game on!

"This is our year! How do you want to be remembered?"

That spring season of 1986, the Northwest Rangers went on a thirty-nine-game winning streak and ranked number one in the country for three weeks at various points of the season. That season set a school record for victories (44-6) in a single season and still holds strong as of 2022. We accomplished our goals as the North Divisional Champions and the eventual Mississippi State champions, and we qualified to host. Unfortunately, the dream season fell apart in the one series playoff in the region. I was elected team captain at the year-end banquet and All-State honorable mention by the Coaches Association. My batting average was 301, and my defense allowed only one pass ball and one error for the entire year. My game continued to improve, and I academically qualified for Memphis State University. I was offered a college baseball scholarship in my hometown to compete in college baseball and get my four-year degree.

As I transferred back to Memphis, I felt the pain of starting over yet again. Just like high school football, I didn't play junior year to start over my senior year. My freshman year, I chose to begin my career at Columbia State, only to transfer to Northwest to start again. Now I was signing with Memphis State for another part of my journey. Looking back, this was extremely hard. I would have to say the most painful part was leaving Northwest after that incredible year and building so many relationships, including those with a top-notch coaching staff. Furthermore, I wanted to be able to fit into a situation where I could grow and be in one place longer than nine months. I was hoping Memphis State would be that place. With my parents in close by Germantown, I felt like it was going to be a perfect fit.

To my delight, after my conclusion at Northwest, I received an invitation to try out for the National USA Team that would compete in the Pan-American games later that year. It was an exciting time because the '88 Olympics in Seoul, South Korea, were right around the corner. I, along with a handful of Memphis players, received tryout invitations. I thought this would offer an incredible opportunity to showcase my skills as a catcher and see how I stacked up with other players around the nation.

The tryouts lasted for two weeks, and I made it through three rounds of cuts before the team decided on two All-American catchers from the West Coast. The National Team was targeting a local player to generate interest, and I felt like I had an outside chance to reside as a bull pen/emergency catcher for the squad. This was not to be because I was released before the final team was chosen. The tryout was a great experience, and I made a regional college team that played the National Squad in a nine-inning contest at Millington's new national baseball facility. The game was ultra-competitive with the local collegiate team beating Team USA by five runs going into the eighth inning. However, Team USA came storming back in the bottom of the ninth to win in dramatic fashion.

My junior year in college would be my last to compete in organized baseball. There comes a time to face that reality and mine happened spring of 1987. When I started school at Memphis State, after the busy and successful summer baseball schedule, my right shoulder flared up with tendonitis once again. As classes and fall baseball were in full force, baseball for me would not happen again until spring. I was now on the disabled list for the fall semester. Looking back, I'm not sure why I didn't get an MRI to look for further damage to my throwing arm or take a medical redshirt.

Years later, after my baseball career was over, I didn't throw a ball of any sort for around ten years. The sabbatical allowed my arm to heal and eventually throw pass routes and drill work as a football coach. Over time, it started to hurt once again, and an MRI indicated tears in my rotator cuff and my shoulder was pretty much bone on bone. I held off surgery, but eventually threw my arm completely out the ensuing season. It was nothing over the top with pain, but a small pop in my shoulder, and that was it. My rotator cuff was officially torn apart. I can throw farther by using my left arm now. Kind of sad.

But going into the spring semester following a fall of rest, I liked my chances to earn the starting catching role. This time, there were three other players fighting for the job. Those guys were good, especially the freshman from Kentucky who had a cannon for an arm. I knew this would be a dog fight for playing time. Perseverance and solid performances in preseason games gave me the inside track leading up to the opener with powerhouse Arkansas in early March. As fate would have it, I won the first start and attempted to throw out a baserunner stealing third in thirty-nine-degree weather. As I released the ball, pain radiated in my right shoulder like no other and I came out of the game immediately.

After sitting out two more months for rehab, I returned for a couple series; however, my arm just wasn't healing, and I made the painful decision of walking away from the game I loved and didn't play my senior year at Memphis. The rollercoaster of multiple rehabs was excruciating and exhausting.

I was finished with that chapter of my life, and depression began to set in.

Now what?

CHAPTER 8

ALONG CAME "POLLY" – "POLLY BETH", THAT IS

ON THE LAST night before I moved out of the athletic dorm, I sat on my bed, contemplating what would happen next in life. Until that very moment, my routine, my schedule, and my existence had been completely mapped out in terms of when to wake up, what to eat, and when to go to class. On some nights, the team had a strict curfew, and *every* day at 7:00 a.m. sharp, we were woken up to the jingle of keys, a loud knock, and then the opening of the door. Coach Armstrong would then yell, "College time!" to motivate players of all sports to get their asses out of bed to go to class. Every aspect in my life was regimented and now I was overcome with all the changes about to take place. That's when my roommate barged in.

"You going to dinner? Last night, they served steak," Forrest Nabors informed me.

"Not hungry," I replied. "I have a ton to do before I leave tomorrow."

"What's the plan, Mike, now that your baseball days are over?"

Nabors didn't pull any punches and got right to the point. He had been like that since grade school.

Now that question hit me like a ton of bricks as the real world was at my doorstep. It took a minute or so to wrap my head around it before I replied, "Nabe, I have a ton on my plate. I need to find a job. You know my parents just moved to Texas; so I need to find a place to live in like one week," I sadly reminded him.

At that very second, I realized the sports bubble that I had lived in throughout my college years was about to burst and the reality of entering the real world was staring me in the face.

Entering the real world was not particularly an easy transition, at least for me anyhow. First, I immediately had to move out of the comfortable confines of the athletic dorm. Next, I moved to my parents' empty house in the suburbs that they had put on the market because my dad took a job in Texas. The good news was it was rent free; the bad news was the house was shown two to three times a week with little warning, and it could be sold at any moment.

During that transitional period, I didn't have time to waste. I had to find a job and new living accommodations while I finished up my business degree. On paper, I was a still a junior and needed to enroll in summer school to make up some ground from multiple school transfers and taking only twelve hours every spring to accommodate a busy baseball schedule.

That next week, I found a job waiting tables and eventually landed a second gig tending a bar at a popular watering hole next to Memphis State campus. Within a couple weeks, I went from a collegiate athlete on scholarship to someone desperately trying to find employment and a place to live.

The following week the house was sold; Dad informed me I had three weeks to find a new place or move to Dallas. The pressure was on. I looked at several places in the meantime; however, I needed a roommate or two to offset some upcoming expenses. That weekend my luck started to change. At least that's what I thought.

During my shift at Newby's Restaurant, I was approached by a casual friend. "I heard you're looking for some roommates."

"Hey, Kathy, good news travels quick. I thought you had a room-mate living in East Memphis," I replied.

"We need a third roomie to offset expenses," she explained. "I thought you might be interested."

It's like she was reading my mind. "I totally understand. Tell me more," I said.

Within another week, I considered living with two "Type A" personalities of the opposite sex. It was a bit different from living with 400 guys in an athletic dorm. We set a few ground rules and made it happen. I thought, because I have two sisters, I could make this work.

During the next few months, the rough transitional period only intensified. For whatever reason, I decided time away from school was what I needed so I took a semester off. Furthermore, my dating life was erratic and counterproductive. Looking back at this period in my life, I should have pursued a licensed therapist to work though my issues. I imagined my pride, not to mention my savings account, were the main obstacles.

After living with my two platonic female roommates for almost a year, I started to have a different and confusing outlook. After a couple of extremely unproductive relationships of my own and witnessing my roommates having their challenges, I decided that it was time to take a break from the dating scene entirely. I felt like my wheels were hopelessly spinning nowhere. I needed to look deep inside and figure out what direction to head in.

For roughly one year, I stepped away from dating and relationships completely. Looking back, I was convinced that I was being pulled in this direction, but I was not quite sure why. My guess: it was my guardian angel readjusting the unproductive path I was on.

At times, I felt like a psychiatrist as I witnessed constant fighting between my roommates. It seemed like the most intense fights started in the kitchen. Questions like: "Did you eat my yogurt?" or "Are you going to wash some dishes?" turned into "Why did you wear my tan blouse without asking me?"

These direct accusations usually would escalate into verbal assaults that would almost become physical. On several occasions, I stepped between them and provided endless counseling to each of them. They were having some transitional issues in life, as well. I strongly considered moving out once the lease was up, but, to my surprise, both decided they could not live another second together and beat me to the punch before the bloodshed started. As a result, I found two more roommates.

My life was changing by the minute, and my hiatus from dating was productive, so I continued my quest for solitude in this area of my life.

As the year rolled on, I continued endless work hours and signed up for a full summer class schedule at Memphis. As summer kicked in, I was working most days and sometimes double shifts. Night or evening classes appealed to my work schedule at Newby's because of the proximity to campus and my report time was at nine p.m. I worked Tuesday, Thursday, and Saturday nights and picked up lunch shifts at Mortimer's. As time went on with the demands of summer school, I ended my time at Mortimer's and concentrated on my shifts that lasted deep into the night at Newby's.

On average, I would make close to 300 bucks a shift, which was incredible money back in the '80s. On paper, it seemed like a wild work/school schedule, but I was able to make serious money and work toward my business degree. Again, my plan to continue a no-dating policy was in effect. I was bound and determined to keep my bachelor ways moving forward.

At least, those were my intentions.

One Sunday afternoon, the evening manager at Newby's, Cliff Garner, called a staff meeting. "Okay, everybody. I'll get to the point: We are down three members of our wait staff. One is taking summer vacation, and two abruptly quit yesterday. Today, while I was eating lunch at Christopher's, I might have found someone that would fit in nicely at Newby's. I'm pretty sure she will join us."

"When?" I asked.

"Your night. Thursday."

Newby's had shown some turnover history with the wait staff because of the late hours and the unruly crowd. The bottom line was that a "thick skin" was needed to be on the floor in the often-packed restaurant with sometimes very drunk customers. On average, we could count on a fight every few nights and customers who would walk out on their tabs were expected. On weekends, we hired a bouncer to help, but it was still an intense job. This job was clearly not for everyone.

As Cliff and I stood behind the elevated bar and looked out into the main dining room, he jumped in. "Okay, O'Neill, the new girl has very little, if any, experience in a restaurant. I need you to come in early and show her the ropes."

"Got it."

"Make sure she knows how to write-up food orders and make highballs. Make sure she understands where all the beer and top-shelf alcohol is and introduce her to Ivan, Henry, Michael, and the rest of the staff when she arrives."

"No problem."

I agreed but was a touch apprehensive because of her lack of experience and knew how stressful a packed restaurant full of intoxicated patrons could potentially be. On the upside, the bar service was easy.

I showed up at Newby's around 7:30 that night to help train our new employee. I called Cliff at home to get an idea when the new girl would arrive. He said anytime. He informed me he thought I would like to work with her. "She is smart and has a great smile. Her name is Beth, and, yes, she is easy on the eyes."

Not sure how to take that. Cliff was in his mid-thirties and had been married a couple times. Cliff, sometimes when he saw a pretty girl at the bar said, "Hey, let me introduce you to my future ex-wife."

That was his go-to line every time. So, I wasn't quite sure of what to make of this. It was almost like he was trying to set me up with someone he just hired. *Slow down*, I thought. *I'm not even back in the market completely.* It was only recently that I started to get back into the dating scene, and I was taking baby steps.

As we hung up the phone, I looked and saw what appeared to be a young lady bent over tying her shoe or picking up something she dropped on the floor in the near-empty front part of the restaurant. After retrieving her dropped car keys, she started walking my way. The first thing I saw was a big, beautiful smile and knew immediately this was the new girl here for her first shift at Newby's. Cliff was correct. She was extremely easy on the eyes with a great smile with some serious '80s hair. I mean the big volume kind with bold curls and a fair amount of hair spray. She was tanned and decked out in cut-off blue jean shorts and a black halter top tied at the waist. My heart skipped a beat as she walked my way and I could barely utter hello before she began talking.

"Hello, I'm Beth Merwin. You must be Mike. I'm your new waitress. Sorry that I'm a bit late. I had a little car trouble, but everything is okay now."

"Hi! That's right; I'm Mike. You're good. No problem at all."

"Wow, this place was hard to find and wasn't sure where to park."

"Yes, parking is tricky, but I'll show you where the employees park, but someone needs to walk you there after your shift to be safe. Never go alone," I said after shaking her hand. "I heard Cliff found you while you were applying at Christopher's."

I already knew Cliff's side of the story but was eager to hear Beth's.

"Yes, I guess Cliff overheard I was looking, and he blurted out that Newby's had an opening. I've never heard of Newby's but was interested. I asked my mom later if I could wait tables at a college bar, and she said okay."

"That's great," I replied. "We need some good help around here, and we could potentially get slammed tonight. Let's get started."

By this time, I began to walk her around the restaurant, bar, and game area for a rather quick orientation. "This is our main dining room, and the room over there has video games, pool tables, and other stuff. That is usually where the fights break out."

"Fights?" she asked with her eyes wide open.

"Just run behind the bar if one starts. Come alert me and stay away from those drunk idiots."

As we began going through the menu and register, I knew she was quick to learn and smart. She asked great questions and had zero problems with mixing basic highballs and figuring out where all the top-shelf liquor and beer were located. She was so eager to learn and so easy to talk with. During that 45-minute training session and going over the basics, I learned that she had graduated from Germantown and just got back from her senior trip. *That explains the tan*, I thought. She informed me that she was ready for anything after I gave her a heads-up on how rowdy things could get in here.

"Just let me know if you need anything, I'll make your shooters." Then, like clockwork, tables began to fill up. "Oh yes, one more thing. The third waitress on duty called in sick only minutes before her shift. Now we have only two working the floor tonight."

She didn't seem phased by this information.

Nine o'clock rolled around and she was already getting busy with five tables as my shift began. By 11:30, Beth and I were getting slammed at the bar, and she was working eight to ten tables. Every now and then, I would ask if she was doing okay, and she just smiled and said, "I'm good."

She was not afraid one bit. Not only was she in the weeds and holding her own, but everyone was talking about the new girl, not only how attractive she was, but how she was a machine working all those tables. I overheard people at the bar asking, "Who is that?"

"How long has she been here? What's her name? Is she dating anyone?" random bar customers would ask.

I saw Cliff out of the corner of my eye, and he walked over to the bar. "So, what do you think of my new hire?"

"You hired a rockstar. What's not to like?" I replied.

"Let's have a celebratory shooter on Newby's to congratulate my hire and welcome Beth to the family," Cliff insisted.

I was breaking one of my own rules of drinking during a shift but at this point I could use one. As Cliff made a round of Rattlesnake shooters, I summoned Beth to join us for a quick shot. As we threw our second shot back, I noticed the guy who would come around taking Polaroids for five bucks a copy. "Would you guys like a picture together?"

"Sure," I said, reaching in my tip jar.

So, we have a picture documenting that first night we worked together. Cliff was in the picture also, but he was eventually cut out by Beth.

It did seem a bit off, but Cliff continued to schedule Beth and me every Tuesday, Thursday, and Saturday nights together. I learned later it wasn't a coincidence. Beth later made the statement that she had been a bit apprehensive when she first started; however, that thinking went out the window as she made close to $300 on her first night. Newby's served as a career trap for some; however, the money was so good that some ditched college or disregarded their degrees to sling whiskey. One of our senior bartenders had an MBA from SMU. He was in his forties.

Over the next couple weeks, Beth and I worked together every shift. As our wait staff returned from their vacations, Beth was able to get some help on the floor. As the summer crowds started to build, I asked Cliff if I could start training Beth to tend bar to help me on extremely busy nights, and he agreed. So, I began the process of training her how to make different cocktails and popular shooters.

"Okay. I've got this," Beth proudly said. "Kamikaze shooter is made up of a half shot of vodka, a half shot of triple sec," she said as she raised both bottles at once and poured, "and then a splash of Rose's lime juice." She then reached for a shot glass, put it on the mat in front of the ice, picked up a large glass, stuck it into shaker, held it up to her shoulder, and gave it a good rattle. She took the glass out of the shaker, put the strainer inside the shaker, and tilted it down for a perfect pour.

"How's that?" she said with a big smile.

"Like an old pro," I said with an even larger smile. "You're ready. You've got this."

I knew it wouldn't take long because she was smart, and it wasn't rocket science. It was obvious that we enjoyed being around each other at work and the idea of asking her out was something I didn't contemplate at the time. Probably because of our age difference. We were almost five years apart as she had just graduated high school and, if I had played my hand right, I would have been a recent college grad by then.

That Saturday night, two weeks after Beth started working at Newby's, I got a call at the bar telling me she would be late again for her shift. More battery issues. At the time, Beth drove a beautiful baby blue Porsche 911. *Damn,* I thought, *time for a new battery. Second time in two weeks.*

"No problem. Can I come get you?"

"No, on the way soon."

"Okay. See you when you get here."

As expected, we were slammed once again. Most college kids going to other schools had made their way back home and wanted to catch up with the locals. Beth came in the crowded bar and immediately was placed in the weeds. It was nonstop the minute she arrived. About two hours into the shift, she came behind the bar.

"Hey, check out the old guy sitting in the booth right next to the bar."

I glanced over, and it was a guy, around thirty, checking us both out.

As she turned her back to the bar and looked directly at me, she explained, "This guy is the person who helped me jump my battery and took it upon himself to follow me to work."

She felt very uncomfortable, especially when this dude asked her out upon arriving.

Without hesitation I said, "Tell this old dude you date the bartender." I reached over for her hand, pulled her close to me, and put my arm around the small of her back. I was selling it. "Tell him if he asks you out again, 'My boyfriend will be pissed off and it's going to get ugly in here.'"

Within minutes, the guy departed before I had to turn into a jealous boyfriend.

As the night wrapped up, I cut Beth from her shift at about three a.m. and told her that I would walk her to her car to make sure the creep was not hanging around. To be honest, I really enjoyed playing the boyfriend role over the past couple hours. During that time, I started to play the "what-if" game in my mind. *What if I ask her out? What if she rejects it? Would it be weird if I date a coworker?*

After we started working together, I really got to know her on a personal level and what a dynamic person she truly was. Along with her obvious beauty, she was a confident and nice person that I could tell had a giant heart. She was not your typical eighteen-year old. I knew I was immature at her age. Beth had a calm demeanor and maturity that wasn't typical for someone her age. She was easy to talk to and I felt like I could be myself when we were together. It seemed like the whole bar thought we were dating, and she later told me she was good with that because of all the guys relentlessly hitting on her during her shifts. It was as though I tried to visualize a relationship with her after the façade we created. To be frank, I wanted to play that role even more.

As promised, at the end of her shift, we made our way to her car, which was parked behind the restaurant. On the way, we conversed casually about our work night and how I would be the made-up boyfriend to ward off potential issues.

"Hey, if you need or want me to step up as the workplace boyfriend, I am available," I said, grinning from ear to ear. "I'm pretty good at it."

"I won't hesitate," she replied.

As she unlocked her door, she turned to say goodbye. I leaned over and our lips found each other. My heart about jumped out of my chest because I felt nothing but complete and unadulterated passion. I had hoped that was the case for her; however, I wasn't so sure she was expecting a kiss by the look on her face. She was caught off guard; but I could feel the passion was mutual. That kiss wasn't planned or thought out whatsoever. After a few more incredible kisses, my mouth gently moved to her right ear. "Would you like to go to dinner next Friday night?" I softly asked.

"I would love that," she said before we continued our passionate kiss.

CHAPTER 9

FIRST DATE NIGHT

MAN, DID WE cover some ground on our first date night. First, she insisted on driving to my house in East Memphis because she told her parents she had a babysitting opportunity that night. Which was partially true because we almost had to move the date because of the babysitting job she had agreed to two weeks prior to me asking her out. About midday Friday, the couple cancelled their plans, and we were able to move forward. She just didn't clue in her parents about the cancelled babysitting task. After she arrived, we took off for downtown. The Memphis Rendezvous restaurant was the destination.

Walking down the back alley in downtown Memphis, the night was full of potential and excitement. The enticing aroma of Rendezvous ribs infiltrated the entire area. Inside, the restaurant was bustling with hungry BBQ-seeking patrons while agile waiters moved their trays of food and pitchers of beer with ease, slicing through the crowded bar and dining room.

"Oh my gosh. This place is packed, and the food smells amazing!" she said.

"Just wait until you get some of those ribs. They serve them dry. This place is world famous, you know."

"Let's start off with a cheese plate," I said as we took our seats on a two-top overlooking the main dining room. As we got familiar within the confines of the restaurant, a conversation I had had with my brother slipped in my mind.

After I popped the question of a possible date last Saturday night, I did a bit of research on Beth Merwin from Germantown High School. The ability to research was obviously much different than today's age of social media. You had to do things by talking to people, and I knew exactly where to begin: Parks! I called my brother, who was about to move back from Dallas, where he just graduated high school. Three years prior my father took a job in Texas, then uprooted my brother and Mom from Germantown. Parks was not a fan of this transfer whatsoever. At Germantown, he was well-connected, extremely popular, and had a girlfriend he had dated for a year and a half. I had called him while he was packing for the big move. Parks was Memphis-bound post-high school, and I would have bet my next month in tips that he knew Beth Merwin.

"Hey, dude. You know a girl named Beth Merwin that went to Germantown that was in your class?"

"Of course, I know her. We were friends. How do you know her?" I could tell he was curious.

"We are coworkers, and I just asked her out."

There was about five seconds of dead air after my last sentence. "What? Really? You know she has a kid?" Parks said.

"Come again. Did you just say she has a child?"

"Yes, back in tenth grade, I believe." He paused. "She hasn't told you yet?"

No, obviously not. After we exchanged a bit more information, we hung up.

Upon absorbing this new information after our phone call, I was even more intrigued and motivated to go out with Beth. Her maturity and calming nature were starting to make sense to me. To be honest, I felt a bit guilty working behind the scenes interrogating my brother, but in hindsight, I truly believed learning about her situation was beneficial to our new relationship, at least from my perspective.

The couple days before our date, I had a chance to reflect and recall her mannerisms and character in a brand-new light. I could sense Beth was kind and extremely focused. Her determination was paramount, and her actions had purpose. The attraction that I had for her was real. Furthermore, the upmost respect of having a child in high school and dealing with all the challenges associated with that began to resonate with me. At that time, I had no clue how many obstacles and challenges she had overcome in her life thus far. I wanted Beth to tell me on her own terms about her sweet daughter.

Our conversation in that crowded restaurant was genuine and flowed naturally. Somehow, the distractions around us were blocked out by getting to know one another. There was no acting, deception, or name-dropping. Just two people who felt completely comfortable in front of one another and enjoyed each other's company. Two people whose immediate goals were not to jump into a serious relationship. I was in the process of resetting my priorities in all aspects of my life; however, Beth's situation was far more complicated when compared to my simple immaturity and a lack of direction.

After a great dinner of Memphis BBQ and engaging conversation, we left downtown and headed to our stomping ground: Newby's. Nothing like heading to work on our night off on the first date, but we had a more important task to handle.

"Let's go public with our first date and do a bit of grandstanding," I said as I took Beth's hand while crossing busy Highland Street to arrive at the entrance of the overpacked bar. There was a nice line we cut in front of while the bouncer checked IDs.

"Are you guys on a date?" inquired the bouncer. "Come right in."

"Thanks, Tiger. Matter of fact, we sure are," I said as we skipped in front of a dozen or so people.

As we weaved through the crowd, Too Tall Todd, the bartender on duty, saw us immediately and made an unscheduled announcement on the spot. "Looks like Newby employees Mike and Beth are on their first date! Don't we have a company policy against that?" he said, grinning from ear to ear.

We both smiled while Beth's face started to blush. "First round on Newby's, you two," Too Tall announced.

As expected, regulars and coworkers were talking about us being seen together. That was fun and felt right. After the free cocktail at the bar, I figured we might get asked to help with a busy bar crowd on that packed Friday night. That wasn't unusual at all. That was not going to happen tonight. Not on our first date. Then it was time to bounce and head to the Half Shell a few miles away where we could hear each other's voices rather than compete with the loud bar scene.

After some talking and kissing under a clear summer sky in the parking lot of the Half Shell, we headed to my house, so she could make the long drive back to Germantown. That's when she just came out and told me while we stood in the circle driveway, "I have a beautiful daughter named Brooke, and I want you to meet her." Next, she began to describe in remarkable detail about what had happened over the past couple years in her life. I mainly listened with an inner peace and was elated that she began to open her world to me.

She didn't leave until almost four a.m. I can't explain it, but I felt an immense peace and ease about getting to know her. We had a perfect first date!

CHAPTER 10

MEET THE O'NEILLS

THE WEEK FOLLOWING our first date just increased my desire to get to know Beth better. As we continued to work and date, it was time to meet sweet Brooke. I wanted to meet her so badly but wasn't exactly sure how to go about it. Often, I would inquire about what Brooke's likes and dislikes were. Our conversations always included updates about Brooke, and I began to get a picture about Beth's life growing up and the challenges and setbacks that accompanied having a child in high school. Compared to my life, she was forced to face reality at the tender age of sixteen versus some kid who had to change their life plan from playing baseball at the age of twenty-one.

She had to sacrifice, plan, deal with humiliation, and hear from people who gave her endless advice about what was the right thing to do given her situation. The extreme advice ranged from giving Brooke up for adoption to abortion. The latter was never an option in Beth's mind and angered her. Her parents wanted her to go six hours away to college to have a so-called "normal college experience." There were so many moving parts to her life, I began to discover.

As our summer romance marched on, we decided to include Brooke. On a whim, I asked Beth if she liked the zoo. Every child liked the zoo. How could I go wrong with this one? The zoo it was!

It was midweek, on a hot summer Memphis day, when Beth brought Brooke over to my house to begin our journey to the Memphis Zoo. When she pulled into the circle drive in front of my house, I could see a little person in the backseat. I waited on the doorstep, sweating profusely. She parked, smiled, and opened the door on the driver's backseat side. By that time, I was moving her way. I saw a precious little girl giving me the biggest smile you could ever imagine. She also had a mouth full of animal crackers with probably the entire box scattered throughout the backseat. Without hesitation, she made a gesture that I would never forget. Brooke, smiling with animal crackers in each hand, extended her right hand out and said, "Cookie."

She just offered me one of her cookies. Who was I to say no? I ate the cookie in one bite. Brooke laughed at me. It melted my heart. She was just perfect, and the zoo date hit the mark! After we returned to the house, she took a two-hour nap to recover from the hot afternoon. Beth and I joined her.

As the summer continued, so did our romance. Between our work schedules and dating, we saw each other almost every day. We both loved music and enjoyed dancing, so we went to concerts on Mud Island and sometimes danced the night away at Incahoots Nightclub. We owned the dance floor as beads of sweat drenched our clothing after eight or so consecutive songs. Neither one of us would back down from the next song; it was a competition to see who would leave the floor first. That summer, she spent most waking hours in my neck of the woods, and I loved it.

Over the 4th of July weekend, we decided to hit the road for a trip to Dallas to meet the parents. This gave us both an opportunity to discuss the big picture of our lives.

"So, what's your game plan? Where do you see yourself in five years?" I quizzed her as if she were applying for a job.

"I think I want to go to law school and be a trial lawyer. I think I'll raise Brooke in a big city, probably somewhere besides Memphis," she quickly answered. "I think I would make a very good attorney. What about you?"

"You would. No doubt. I want to go into business, I guess, sales of some sort. I was approached to teach and coach in high school not long ago, but those people don't make enough money. After I get my business management degree, I'll start interviewing and see where that takes me." I still wasn't confident about the direction I was going in at the time.

While pulling into my parents' driveway off Chimney Hill Lane in Richardson, Texas, my anticipation and anxiety levels continued to rise.

"Mom, Dad, meet Beth," I said thirty seconds after we stopped in front of the house. I guess they were anticipating our meeting also as they had made their way out the front door. It had been over two months since I'd seen them since they moved. "The house looks great."

"Hello Mr. and Mrs. O'Neill," Beth eagerly said. "It's great to meet both of you."

As we headed inside, she added, "Wow! It smells delicious in here."

About that time, my sister, Liz, and my brother-in-law, Jimmy, pulled into the back ally driveway.

"Mikey, what's happening? How was your trip?" Liz inquired.

"Big Ron, what's for dinner?" Jimmy said as he looked under a cast iron skillet and opened the oven. "Looks like Tex-Mex of chalupas and taco al carbon with refried beans and green chilis."

"That's right, asshole! Hands off," Dad warned. He just broke the cussing ice, and it happened within minutes of arrival. I did warn her.

To be honest, I wasn't quite sure which direction this would go. For the most part, I kept girls I dated away from the house because my dad could be a loose cannon when it comes to conversation. I loved him, but his sense of humor, one-liners, and colorful language could take some time to get used to. She rolled with the punches.

Early on, the dinner was pleasant, and the conversation was productive and informative. The particulars were covered, mainly by Mom and Liz. "Where is your family originally from? What do you want to study in school? Did you know Parks when he went to Germantown?"

As Dad casually leaned over in Beth's direction, he said, "You know Mike dated some real racehorses over the years." As I slowly shut my eyes, shaking my head in disgust, I thought, *here we go*. My mom was mortified while Jimmy began to snicker.

Beth's reply was epic, as if she'd had an hour to think of a response about that obnoxious statement. "Well, Ron, *I* have been known to win a race or two myself over the years."

That line completely broke any tension may have been in the dining room that evening, and the long holiday weekend was off to a great start.

"You tell him, Beth," Mom said before giggling.

During that trip to Dallas over the 4th of July, Beth and I began to consider what would life hold for us down the road. Was this simply more than a summer romance? Could we handle a long-distance relationship?

"How will you feel being six hours away from Brooke when you take off to Knoxville?" I asked.

She calmly replied, "It's going to be extremely hard, so I need to graduate in record time. I need an incredible degree so I can make a great living and support my Brooke. How do you feel about dating me after finding out I have a child?"

"You having a child doesn't sway my thinking about you at all. It only intensifies my feelings. I want to make this work, Beth, even when you take off for school. Looks like I'll be coming to Knoxville quite often if you can fit me in your busy college schedule."

"You bet I will. You better come up all the time," she said.

Upon our return, summer school and work were at the top of my agenda. In between summer classes and work, Beth spent more and more time at my house. Beth too decided to enroll in the second summer session. Now our schedules were almost identical. Often, I would catch her reading through her notes from class for a possible quiz or finishing up a paper the next day. All this while working a shift at Newby's.

"How can you do that?" I asked.

"Do what?" she replied.

"Remember or concentrate in between waiting tables."

"When else am I going to do it?"

She was a motivated and driven person. I knew I needed to up my game, and that's exactly what I did because it was beyond time for me to wrap up my business management degree from Memphis.

Beth was also on a mission. She was exploring the possibilities of practicing law at some point or obtaining an accounting degree and achieving her CPA. Her goal was to have Brooke on her own upon the completion of her studies, and there wasn't a second to spare.

At that time, her parents were raising Brooke and were doing a sound job; however, I could sense somewhat of a power struggle between the two parties. Beth was focused on obtaining a degree and banking some money with the goal of branching out and raising Brooke without relying on her parents, while staying somewhat social and normal for someone at the tender age of eighteen. I marveled at how focused she was. She would constantly remind me, "I need to make Brooke a part of this decision."

CHAPTER 11

80-85

WHEN THE SUMMER of '89 began, Beth will say even now that she was in no position whatsoever to begin a lasting romance; it didn't even cross her mind. She just graduated high school, had a fifteen-month old, and was going to college. Fitting in an older boyfriend was not exactly in the playbook. I guess, however, the same could be said from my point of view; I didn't anticipate dating while trying to get my life together. The cards were overwhelmingly stacked against us before she ever walked through the doors at Newby's Restaurant. I guess you could say true love would not be denied. The only things we had in common at that moment were an open heart and the ability to take a chance on the passion we felt for each other.

One night, I cooked her dinner at my house and decided to pitch a tent in the backyard under the stars on an unusually cool summer night. After a couple bottles of merlot, I leaned over for a kiss and noticed she had nodded off while curled up in the sleeping bag.

I softly said, "I love you."

Without hesitation, her head popped up, she and said, "I heard that! I love you too."

As August was fast approaching, I realized that the school year would begin soon. In my mind, I was preparing myself for a long-distance relationship with my "freshman-in-college girlfriend." The countdown toward fall weighed heavily on my mind while my love only grew stronger. Personally, I had grown so much by being involved in a "real relationship." A relationship that required me to be unselfish and focused on not only one individual, but two. In time, I knew 100 percent Beth would reach those goals she set forth for her young family, and now I started to picture how I would factor into her busy life. So, I kept my heart open, and Beth did the same.

As the summer was winding down, we were spending the better part of every day in each other's company while our bond of love and friendship continued to blossom. Fighting and arguments were not in our DNA. Everything about our bond just felt right. I'm not quite sure who started our motto, but it went like this: "Hey, when I'm eighty, you will be eighty-five."

Over time, we have shortened it to 80-85. One thing is for certain, I damn sure want to hold up my end of that bargain!

CHAPTER 12

WHEN THE GOING GETS TOUGH, THE TOUGH GET GOING

AS THE SUMMER of my romance with Beth continued, life was about to change dramatically. Mid-August approached, and Beth was gearing up for orientation at the University of Tennessee. She had picked one of the last sessions before school started that fall. The plan was to go to orientation with her parents and Brooke, get her class schedule, look at the possibility of going through rush or other activities, and come back to Shelby County after three days. I could sense Beth was hesitant about the trip, but she kept her thoughts concealed. She had multiple things on her mind and taking off to Knoxville for a semester without her daughter was severely weighing on her. She spoke a few times about the challenge of taking off and wanted to maybe investigate Memphis State to pursue her degree while raising Brooke nearby. Her parents, however, kept insisting that she needed to pursue her degree and enjoy the college experience while they cared for Brooke back in Germantown. Beth was struggling with this, and she considered different options for her future.

Orientation came and went. Upon the return home, with a class schedule and possible extracurricular activities to balance out her college experience during her freshman year, she beelined it over to East Memphis. Upon arrival, she was happy to see me, but I could tell she was conflicted.

After a quick kiss and pleasantries, she spoke up, "I cannot and will not go to Knoxville this fall."

Personally, I took that as good news, but I knew there was much more to it than us preserving a long-term relationship. This was a surprising turn of events; however, I was sold on the fact she would be a Tennessee Vol in a couple short weeks, but I was mistaken.

That evening, Beth explained that she had been thinking about her plans ever since Brooke was born. She was open to her parents' idea of going off to school and acting like a normal college kid for a period while pursuing her degree and then pick up her life with Brooke in four years. She honestly considered this path and wanted to experience the orientation to see if she would have a change of heart. The answer was crystal clear: No. She then thought about the monumental task of sharing her revelation with her parents on I-40 heading home but just could not pull the trigger.

"Sit down," I said as I held her hand, pulling her next to me on the living room couch. "Let's talk about how this plays out."

"I'm afraid to tell my parents about staying home and ditching Knoxville while going to school in Memphis," she said as her voice rattled. Beth was clearly upset. I had not seen her this shaken up before. "I'm worried, Mike. I'm concerned they won't understand at all." By this time, tears were beginning to form in her pretty eyes.

"Surely, your parents will understand your motivation in making this decision, and they will be more than happy to accommodate your wishes."

Again, that was my perception about how this would unfold. Boy, I was way off.

Beth informed her parents the next morning of her plans to attend Memphis State University and help raise Brooke in the process. She explained that being six hours away would cause endless worry, and she simply could not endure the separation. Her parents' plan was to make several trips in their RV to Knoxville.

Her news wasn't well received in the least bit, and the response to Beth's announcement changed the course of her life. Their response was: "Well, if you are going to go to Memphis, you can pay for it yourself. By the way, you will find another place to live and leave your car in the driveway. You have three weeks, and Brooke will stay here. You can visit, but you need to figure out your living arrangements and plan for paying for school by yourself as well as your transportation situation."

By late morning, she pulled into my driveway extremely upset and confused about how the conversation went down earlier that Monday morning. Upon arrival, she told me how the news was received and all the stipulations set forth.

"The bottom line is, I'm getting kicked out in three weeks, Mike!"

I couldn't believe what she was explaining to me. It's like all the air was sucked out of the room. I just couldn't wrap my mind around how her parents could think like that. While I received particulars of the conversation and her reaction, I could sense her wheels were turning once again. She would not be wearing Tennessee blaze orange that fall. She was clearly upset and bewildered, but she was already getting her plan in motion about her next move.

"What do apartment rentals go for and how does that work?" she asked. "How much do used cars go for? Where is the best place to buy one?"

Again, this was before the internet allowed anyone to shop at any given time, so old school research had to be done. Newspapers, magazines, and real estate publications were the most reliable sources.

On-site research and negotiations had started by early afternoon. We visited multiple apartment complexes that offered immediate living arrangements so we could gauge availability and cost. We kept hearing, "Sorry. We cannot help you, Ms. Merwin. You don't have a credit history."

We kept moving no matter how bad the news was, while she continued to knock items off the to-do list. Beth has always had a continuous, never-ending to-do list.

Next, we took a quick trip to Memphis State University to apply for the fall semester with the hope that it was not too late for her to be admitted. Now this was my territory, and I provided her a quick tour after she applied. The next day, we were back in my car, dropping off applications at various businesses to explore potential employment that would accommodate her new schedule. We were covering major ground.

That afternoon, we stopped at several dealerships on Covington Pike and Mt. Moriah and evaluated various reliable cars that would meet her needs to get around town and transport Brooke safely. I remember we walked for hours in various car lots and looked for the right vehicle.

Beth did not sit around and feel sorry for herself. She was upset, but this fueled her on every single front. That Monday, she chose fight over flight.

The first and most obvious task was to find a place to live. The challenge here was that she was only eighteen and didn't have any history of renting or credit, not to mention limited funds saved. The current funds saved was simple spending money in Knoxville as she began life as a student. However, we found out that her attempts to lease a rental contract was simply not going to happen. That very day, the prospect to rent resulted in five attempts with five denials. I guess you can say it was the process of elimination.

We started in midtown and made our way back east to Germantown with zero luck. The next two days, the results were the same.

We desperately ran around to multiple complexes to no avail. The freshman dorm at Memphis was considered but lost steam as she was emphatic about not having a roommate so Brooke could come and go without issues.

As we continued the hopeless search for an apartment, I felt the need to take some ownership. I was motivated to help in any way possible and wanted to face this challenge together. I followed Beth's lead and jumped in with both feet. As the search continued, we knew logistically picking a safe area in between school and Brooke was a priority. Later, we would figure out transportation that was reliable and safe for her and her toddler. As the full court press continued in the relentless search for accommodations without any results, I boldly asked her, "Why don't you just move in with me? My roommates won't have any problems in finding another roomie to sublease after my departure. No better time than the present. Let's get that one bedroom back in Germantown we saw. It is in a perfect location between school and Brooke."

She began to cry. "Really?"

"Yes."

"Let's do it."

Thankfully, our luck started to change. A one bedroom became available at the last minute, and we moved into Whispering Oaks on that following Friday. Also, because Beth had started taking courses back in June, getting admitted into the fall semseter was a piece of cake. With two hurdles completed, two more were to be conquered: finding future employment and transportation were the next priorities during this wild August of '89.

By this time, the keys to the baby blue Porsche were now in the hands of her dad, as promised, and I was her only source of transportation. Since we were freshly moved in together, this was no issue but knew soon she needed a reliable car. The search ended with a Volvo station wagon that we found at a car dealership in Memphis. Job applications were distributed in between running around looking for apartments and seeking out transportation. Along with working her three nights at Newby's, she received an offer from the Ruby Tuesday restaurant in Germantown and a jewelry store located a couple stores down in the same mall complex. Within three weeks, Beth was working three jobs, taking fifteen hours, and now had a new roommate. We decided to go in all the way and open a joint savings/checking account to manage everything together financially. This commitment was now a joint effort in every aspect and love was the bond.

As we continued to get settled in our ever-changing new world, one thing was abundantly clear. Our commitment and love only grew more intense and stronger through this process. I clearly witnessed what a strong, determined person she was. Beth was unequivocally unselfish in wanting to raise her daughter and dedicated those efforts to build a foundation in order to do so.

It was time for me to wrap up school and obtain a real job. I was at a good point in my life to take on more responsibility and hit our goals as a couple. I had certainly wasted enough time in the transitional phase that included unproductive relationships that went nowhere. I came to the realization that I had found someone who had tremendous faith in God and someone who wasn't afraid to work and achieve their goals. No matter what, the lessons and obstacles I dealt with in terms of sports and school provided a foundation for the challenges Beth and I were now facing. Beth, on the other hand, was simply learning on the fly. Her days as a careless teenage kid came to a halt when she became pregnant in her sophomore year of high school. She had to adjust, accommodate, and commit her efforts in the future to ensure her personal and career goals would be met in due time.

Constantly, she was on the move. She was burning the candle at both ends. Her drive and commitment were unparalleled, which inspired me completely!

As summer changed to fall, our busy lives were in the fast lane. Between work, school, and Brooke, we were making things happen. Also, we weren't completely honest with Beth's parents either when it came to living arrangements. On the surface, her parents thought she was able to sign a lease for the apartment in Whispering Oaks. Unfortunately, we were backed into a corner with mounting expenses that now included an apartment lease, car payments, and tuition that was due before the semester began. Most of the everyday items came from my existing house, but we certainly didn't have everything we needed for the both of us. In a short period, we jointly bought some household goods and some furniture to live comfortably in our new one-bedroom apartment. Still, to this day, I'm not quite sure if they picked up on Beth's living arrangement with me.

One thing that wasn't factored into our new routine was sleep. This was the sacrificial lamb. As Beth started her new work and school schedule, I was still taking night classes and working the graveyard shift at Newby's. We both realized that my Newby's income was the cash cow of this partnership, and we could not switch gears to accommodate a new schedule until I was out of school with my first real job. At times, we found ourselves coming and going. This was one of the most stressful and challenging times in our lives. With all the demands of our young adulthood, we carved out time for each other and Brooke. Weekends were a time to catch up, and Sunday provided quality time for the three of us. Usually, on Saturday nights while I worked, Brooke and Beth were able to have bonding time in our busy world.

The fall of '89 was a complete blur with our busy schedule, which also included me helping the eighth-grade football program. In the spring of '90, it only accelerated. For me, I was taking eighteen hours that spring with summer school on the horizon with no margin for error. Again, the plan for graduation and employment were paramount, and I spent plenty of time in the placement office to sharpen my interview skills. The entire time I was heading for the home stretch, I knew I wanted to make Brooke and Beth permanent in my life, and my urgency only intensified my plan of saving money for an engagement ring and putting together a plan to pop the question.

Unfortunately, Beth and her parents were yet to be on the same page when it came to Brooke. Even today, it's still painful to talk about and never brought up between Beth and her parents. I understand that Miles and Polly had an element of frustration on their side and they felt it was in Beth's best interest to come to their understanding on how to approach her college years. Regrettably, there was very little, if any, compromise, and the two parties continued to move in separate directions when it came to Brooke. Beth's frustration was apparent, but how to get her parents on the same page was deemed to be almost impossible.

As our lives were as busy as ever with the prospects of a bright future, more stress and anguish were on the horizon. About the time I was to graduate in the summer of 1990, Beth's father decided to take an international job at FedEx to fly the MD-11 out of Anchorage, Alaska. This was yet another setback in Beth's journey to have Brooke on her own. Beth clearly didn't have the financial means to keep Brooke in Tennessee with her intense school and work schedule and needed her parents more than ever to help with Brooke until she was able to do so. However, the move to Alaska was now set for the fall of '91, and training had already begun to fly this aircraft. That plan was set in motion three months before Beth was notified of this. It was time to make some major adjustments.

CHAPTER 13

PARTY OF THREE, PLEASE

ETH'S PARENTS LEAVING for Alaska and taking Brooke was not in the game plan at all. The only saving grace was that we had some time to plan and make some adjustments. At the time, the news was excruciating and left deep wounds that took some years to overcome.

Money was on the forefront of our thoughts. Quite simply, Beth needed to save more money to accommodate a child. A plan to accelerate beyond this roadblock was put into motion. With Brooke out of the picture for a while, the one-bedroom apartment was not necessarily moving forward. Incidentally, my lease at Whispering Oaks was almost up when the Merwin's made the announcement to transfer. So, after Christmas, to save money, Beth moved into the dorm at Memphis and I moved in with my grandmother, who could use help around the house. The dorm would be far less money and my grandmother's house was free. Her plan to continue to load up school hours and work as often as possible was in motion.

After graduating Memphis State in the summer of 1990, I was

able to land my first sales job with the Terminix Corporation. I figured out early that with taking a first real job, I would have to take a slight pay cut compared to my bartending gig. However, the opportunity to obtain full health benefits was crucial for a young growing family. I did pass on a couple opportunities that would have required a possible transfer soon, but I understood I needed to be in the same city with Beth while she was grinding through school while working multiple jobs. For the next couple of years, Memphis was where we need to reside.

To supplement my income, I kept my Saturday night shift at Newby's for extra cash to save for an engagement ring. I was almost there, but I knew I needed to shorten my timeline to make this happen. During that time, I was able to fit in coaching eighth grade football. The practices were after work late in the afternoon, and the season, compared to the demands of high school, were relatively minimal. Football kept me balanced during those days.

In the grand scheme of things, our plans were predicated on a wedding date. That year had moved unusually fast, and I had saved enough money for a ring I hoped Beth would love.

On a Saturday night in the winter of 1990, my plan was to secretly ask Miles for Beth's hand in marriage. I arrived on the Merwin's doorstep, ready for anything. "Come in, Mike," Polly said with open arms.

As I made my way inside, I was offered a glass of red, which I gladly accepted. In all likelihood, I could have consumed an entire bottle.

"Miles, can we go in the living room? I would like to have a word with you," I said as I took a second pull from the glass. "Can you excuse us, Polly?"

"Sure, Mike."

Subsequently, we settled on the couch, and I didn't waste a second. "Mr. Merwin, I would like to ask you if I could take your daughter's hand in marriage. I will take extremely good care of her and be a loving father to Brooke," I said while I grinned.

Without hesitation, he responded, "We would be delighted if you proposed to Beth. Polly and I were anticipating this conversation."

"Thank you."

Over the next week, I plotted my proposal.

One evening, I returned to the apartment while attempting to carry out an award-winning acting performance. Beth was making dinner.

"Hey, it's been a long semester. What if I took you to a nice French restaurant in midtown to celebrate the end of another intense semester and you becoming a junior? Maybe meet some friends later in the night?" I asked somewhat nonchalantly, hoping the possibility of hanging out with friends might throw off the scent. "Let's dress up."

"Sure, that sounds lovely," she said, smiling. "Which friends?"

Dang, I thought, *she* had *to go there*. However, I was able to rattle off three couples.

Justine's French Restaurant was one of my grandparents' favorite places to dine when they were younger. My mother's parents adored this high-end French cuisine eatery and went there almost weekly.

That night was my first time to step foot in the door. When we pulled up, valet parking was my only choice to park. It was my first time for that also. Good thing I brought an ample supply of cash. Upon entering Justine's, another pleasant surprise was a coat check. Man, this place was fancy! When I was younger, we just didn't go to places that would valet your car or check your coat.

Beth's face lit up as we entered the elegant restaurant. *Could she be on to me?* Either way, it didn't really matter. The plan was set in stone.

Beth was absolutely stunning in a beautiful strapless gold dress and heels, which complemented her gorgeous flowing blonde hair. Her style was impeccable as we sauntered toward our reserved table; heads were turning. *This is our night*, I optimistically thought.

The atmosphere was perfect! They granted my request for a somewhat isolated table. Within minutes, we enjoyed escargot and French onion soup before a five-course dinner that ended with a baked Alaska and crème brulé. The second after the waiter cleared the remains of the baked Alaska, I nervously fumbled for the ring in my suit jacket. I retrieved it, without saying a word, stood up, and then took a knee right in front of her. She was confused at first and then she began to tear up. While tears were running down her face, she carried a giant smile with it. I had a pretty good feeling the outcome would be favorable.

"Make me the happiest guy in the world. Will you marry me?"

"Yes," she softly replied.

I began to tear up at that moment. What a night. It turned out perfect!

The plan to exchange vows was set and the future was bright. The topic of setting a date was on the agenda. Because I asked her at the end of 1990, ample time was needed for our celebration. We both wanted a big wedding to celebrate our unity, but quickly found out this would take time and planning to accomplish this. In the past, her parents had eloped as well as her brother and his wife. We wanted our wedding to be large and tell the world we were becoming united. The timeline for dates was being explored. First, a spring wedding was much too early with most venues spoken for. To get the church of your choice, you needed at least six months heads-up to make that happen.

Sitting at the kitchen table, we both were fixated on the calendar in sheer silence, not a word for close to five minutes. As I pointed to a date in October, she said, "Nope. The church is not available that weekend."

As we looked at the calendar, we agreed summer was too hot to enjoy the type of gathering we wanted. After looking at several fall dates, we decided on November 2 of that year. Beth always said that I agreed to this date because of the middle school season; however, she was taking eighteen hours of school, and by that time, the semester had a bit of flexibility to take a week off for a honeymoon following our nuptials. Also, the church we targeted was booked until late October. That was our date.

The Catholic church we were patiently in line for had some very special meaning attached. The reason was my mom and dad were married there back in 1959, and it was the oldest Catholic congregation in Memphis with construction starting in 1852. Our plan was to continue this tradition.

To say we were busy in those days leading up to our wedding date would certainly be an understatement. The guest list was on the large side, with more than 300 people in attendance. With all the busyness of planning this large wedding, venues, invitations, and rehearsal dinner coordination was in full effect. Like most brides, Beth took the reins of planning and organizing while taking a full load at Memphis, while I was knee-deep in my first real job as well as feeding my passion to coach middle school and grinding through another season.

The night of November 2, 1991, was unseasonably cold for that time of year, most of the day was in the mid-twenties. This beautiful church in downtown Memphis was the perfect location to obtain the sacrament of marriage on this November evening. Inside the cathedral, the sight of lovely flowers and the smell of frankincense transcended throughout the congregation.

I stood at the altar in my black tux with tails, sporting white gloves, while beads of sweat formed on my upper lip and forehead with the anticipation of my bride coming through those front doors of the church. As Dad (the best man) and I stood in front of the large gathering, it was game time, and the church was silent until "Pachelbel's Canon in D" began to play, and at that distinct moment, my heart filled with contentment. As the procession started act one, I glanced over at Dad as he gave a vote of confidence. "You've got this, son," he said with a nod.

The wedding procession was quite large, and after twelve pairs made their way to the main front of the church, Brooke Whitney took over the show in her adorable flower girl dress. She proceeded about one mile per hour down the aisle, grabbing one flower petal per step. It was the cutest sight ever. Everyone in attendance loved it. However, the one thing that stands out to me more than anything was to see my future bride as the doors opened at the back of the church. As my heart fluttered and my eyes teared up, I could feel the presence of God throughout the entire service, and it started the second those doors were opened to reveal my beautiful Elizabeth.

As my bride walked to the altar, she was on point. Her nerves appeared under control compared to me fighting mine. She leaned over and said, "Hi, handsome. I love you," as she glanced at my sweaty forehead.

After our beautiful nuptials that included a full church service with communion, the wedding party headed over to the 19th Century Club for a night of celebrating and dancing to the sounds of one of our favorite local bands—The Blue Beats.

The next morning, we drove to a cold St. Augustine, Florida, to spend our honeymoon. Unfortunately, it was a bittersweet time for the newlyweds. The night of the wedding, we said our goodbyes to Brooke with her parents before their journey to Alaska. Their plan was to drive their RV up to Anchorage. That would take them almost three weeks to complete. Those goodbyes were excruciating, and our eleven-hour drive from Memphis to St. Augustine was filled with both excitement and disappointment.

In a couple very long months following our return from Florida, we made plans to make a two-week journey to Alaska to accomplish two important tasks: (1) to check on and reconnect with Brooke and see how the family was adjusting to Alaska, and (2) to make an announcement that wasn't guaranteed to be received with open arms. We would hold nothing back.

During the past year of wedding prep, we also met with an attorney that specialized in family law to see what the timeline and process would be for me to officially (with proper legal capabilities) adopt Brooke and join Beth in being the legal guardian of Brooke.

After a few meetings, phone calls, and a trip downtown, I adopted Brooke. "We did it," she proclaimed. "You're Brooke's daddy. You're on her birth certificate. It's official."

"We have one thing left to do: let's go get her," I happily said.

So, planning for a beautiful wedding wasn't the only thing happening in the preceding months leading up to our nuptials. So now, the question was not if Brooke was coming back to Tennessee, but exactly when would that take place.

The trip to Alaska went as planned. After a brief stop in Seattle, we boarded Alaska Airlines with another long flight before we touched down. Beth was smiling from ear to ear the entire trip knowing she would be face-to-face with our sweet daughter. We were apprehensive but carried so much hope and excitement on our journey. As we touched down at Ted Steven Anchorage International Airport, the anticipation and excitement began to take over.

As we deboarded the plane, we just couldn't believe this point in our journey had arrived. While grabbing a piece of luggage in the overhead bin, I noticed Beth start to cry. She had been smiling since we took off from Seattle. "I'm okay. It's a happy cry," she said as she gathered herself.

My heart was filled with love, and minutes later, we were united with Brooke at gate thirty-nine.

Experiencing Alaska in the middle of winter was not only beautiful but created an opportunity to experience another world that included incredible scenery and wildlife.

Upon arriving at their condominium after the twenty-minute drive from the airport, Miles said, "Look behind us," as we pulled in the parking lot. Beth and I turned around at once to witness three moose in all their glory only feet behind the rear bumper.

"These moose are like dogs here in the city of Anchorage. They're everywhere," Miles added. "You can only hunt them in the month of September, but it's extremely hard to get a permit."

We weren't inside longer than ten minutes before Beth cut to the chase. "Mom, Dad, we need to have a talk."

As we stood inside the kitchen, we broke the news. Miles and Polly listened intensely. Beth explained the legal process we endured with a possible timeline set in place. Overall, it was well received, and I truly believe at some point they were anticipating this day would happen, but you could tell by their reaction, it was much faster than they probably anticipated. It was agreed that in early spring Brooke would return to Memphis just after we purchased our first house in the Cordova area. Everything went as planned, and our reunion only intensified the love among our sweet, young family.

CHAPTER 14

IN THE PURSUIT OF PROFESSIONAL HAPPINESS

COMING OUT OF high school in the mid-80s, very little thought was put into what I wanted to do on a long-term basis. Baseball was the immediate plan, and I couldn't convince myself to look at things in the long run. In the back of my mind, sales could be an option but that was way down the road, and I was completely shortsighted about this facet of my life.

My goal now was to work for a Fortune 500 company in sales and move up the company ladder. Also, while looking at different industries and what they paid, I was encouraged about possible earning potential across the board. Evaluating different industries, I found out salespeople can potentially make or earn the most money in the firm outside of top executives and upper-level management, especially if they didn't cap the earnings potential or commission. Back in the late '80s and early '90s, financial industries like selling stocks/bonds or hustling pharmaceuticals or medical devices were highly sought after.

Some companies had terrific benefits that included excellent retirement programs or stock options. If a company was doing well, stock options were a great way to build wealth.

Understanding the earnings potential, benefits, and the flexibility that outside sales rep job offered, I was now motivated to pursue a great job and work my way up. My goal was to start working for a manufacturer with a good salary, potentially with a bonus/commission plan based on performance. In the meantime, score a company car with an expense account to entertain customers. Sounds great, right? My mindset was money is king, and I needed to make a stack of it.

One consistent thing in my busy life during all this transition was football. As I began coaching middle school football, I believed that I could do this anywhere at just about any age, for as long as I enjoyed it. I truly felt that coaching kids in middle school was my calling. I enjoyed that age group because of their curiosity to learn and their will to be motivated. Working with the junior high Red Devils provided balance and meaning to my life.

When I began working at Terminix, practice began at 5:30 p.m., and I would race from my territory, quickly change into my coaching gear, and coach my butt off. The year leading up to our wedding was compiled with Beth's school and work schedule; I hesitated to go through with coaching that season; however, she insisted that I continue to coach. She felt like coaching football was just part of me.

The first year I coached with Skippy Brewer at Kirby Middle School before we were invited to run the Germantown Middle School program, Beth helped me motivate the Kirby players when we played Germantown for a spot in the middle school championship title game. Beth ironed on numbers to bandannas for each player on the roster to be distributed on game day; furthermore, we decided to create and hang banners in the middle of the night to inspire the players. It was two a.m. in our apartment when we finished the last banner.

"What now?" she said.

"Let's hang them," I said.

"Now?"

"No better time than the present. I want my guys see them when they get off the bus heading to class first thing."

It turned into a covert operation to Hickory Hill, and after fifteen banners were hung at Kirby Middle, we were back in bed by 3:30 a.m. Some of the banners read, "Germantown is #1" and "G'Town will crush the Cougars." Of course, we kept it clean with no foul language. The goal was intended for our players to see them before school and be completely hyped up before kickoff. Beth and I never told a soul, even to Brewer or the rest of the coaching staff.

On game night, the players came out smoking and performed with impressive fashion. As I paced the sidelines, our guys had that look in their eyes. They were playing with purpose and physicality. It was almost as if they were playing with a huge chip on their shoulders. The score wasn't even close. I saw Beth in the stands while the team headed toward the locker room after the first half was concluded. She gave me a thumbs-up with a huge smile. She too was convinced our secret plan made the difference.

After the game, I asked a couple players if they noticed any banners when they arrived at school. I only received raised eyebrows and kids shaking their heads in utter confusion. Later, I overheard one school official talking about the banners that were taken down before the kids arrived at school. Damn! You could've fooled me. These guys played pissed off and won by thirty points. We never told anyone about our team banners that night.

After Beth and I were married in 1991, the next fall, Coach Brewer and I were back at Germantown. That year, we had another championship team, and the varsity staff invited us to work the press box on Friday nights. Now, this took it to a whole new level. It was great to be back at Germantown and serve my alma mater once again. It wasn't until that middle school season that I even entertained the thought of coaching at the high school level.

After a couple of seasons back and working the press box on Friday nights, I was asked by Ernest Chism, the long-term principal at Germantown High School, to come in for a meeting during school hours. No problem. By this time, I had changed companies and was selling industrial packaging for a company named The Greif Bros. Corporation. Because I had flexibility, I stopped by the school around lunch time. I went to the main office and was told to have a seat outside of Mr. Chism's office. Strangely enough, I felt like I was right back in high school about to get lit up for something I did. This never happened, but it sure felt like it. After about a five-minute wait, his secretary allowed me to enter his office and shut the door behind me.

As I sat directly across from Mr. Chism, I could not help but think of coming over to his house to hang out with his son, George. George and I were good friends, and he gave me a ride to school my ninth-grade year before I could drive. While in the middle of memories, he interrupted me with a stern handshake and told me to have a seat.

"Thanks, Mr. Chism."

Before I could say anything else, he got right to the point and began to talk.

"Mike, Coach Netherland and I agree that your destiny is to coach at the high school level and teach a subject that would match your major."

About that time, Coach Netherland walked into the office. After making pleasantries, he basically said the same thing. He went on to say, "Mike, you're a natural coach that possesses leadership and motivation. These kids respond and respect you on the highest level."

I was floored and almost speechless. These guys weren't exactly lining up ex-Germantown players to get them to join their coaching staff; that wasn't their style. Usually, they had the pick of the litter when it came to hiring more assistant coaches and usually fished out of the three-state area for prospects. As they continued to speak, the first thing that popped in my mind was teaching. In order to pull this off, I had to teach. My train of thought was going a mile a minute from annual salary to benefits for a young family.

"What's your undergraduate degree in?" Mr. Chism asked.

"Business management," I replied.

"Fine, we offer several business courses here at Germantown."

Back to graduate school to teach and probably make far less money. I had a ton of questions I wanted to ask, but before I could get them out, Mr. Chism offered this: "Mike, if you can coach, you can teach! It's the same concept. Either you're on the field or in the classroom. It's as simple as that. I have been watching you on the field; you're a natural. Next week, I want you to meet with Dr. Setterlund, our assistant principal, and he can give you an idea what it would take to get certified and later get your master's degree."

"Yes, sir. Thank you for the meeting."

As I walked out of the school, I couldn't believe what I had just heard. I was overcome with gratitude and started to think about the possibility of becoming a high school football coach.

That next week, after the varsity team left the practice field, Coach Netherland came to the middle school practice to inform me that Mr. Chism had arranged a meeting with Dr. Setterlund and would like me to come by tomorrow if possible. *Wow,* I thought. *These guys are working fast and must be serious about the conversation we had the week prior.* I knew now I was actively being recruited.

For the second consecutive week, I showed up at the main office of my alma mater to discuss the prospects of teaching at Germantown High school. This time with Vice Principal Tim Setterlund. Dr. Settlerlund joined the administration after I had graduated from Germantown. He had an incredible reputation as an upcoming young administrator. It was only a matter of time until he oversaw a high school.

"Take a seat, Mike," Doc instructed me. "Mr. Chism and Coach Netherland speak highly of you. Let's get down to business and check out your undergraduate transcripts and understand what it would take to qualify as a licensed teacher in the state of Tennessee based on your BA degree."

The meeting was informative, yet overwhelming, as I listened intensely as he basically laid it out for me based on my transcripts he had freshly reviewed. In a nutshell, after one full year of taking general education and business education courses, I could earn my license and begin teaching. After I earned another fifteen to eighteen hours the following year, I could achieve my master's degree. Looking at both routes in becoming a teacher, the master's program was the best choice in the long run. The master's program could provide much better income throughout a possible education career.

"This is the latest eighteen-year period pay scale based on education level and service," he said as he handed me a hard copy of information. "The second page provides an overview of the retirement program based on twenty-five, thirty, and thirty-five years of service."

Overall, our meeting was extremely productive. But for now, I had an overwhelming amount of information I needed to digest and consider the prospects long-term of living on a teacher's salary.

On the professional flip side, I just started my second sales job with Greif Bros., calling on industrial accounts and selling steel, plastic, and fiber drums to prospects within a 150-mile radius of Memphis. With a substantial raise in salary and a new company car, I decided to leave Terminix to join them because of the raise in salary and better long-term prospects. At the time, I felt like the pursuit of becoming a teacher would set our family financial prospects back, and I just couldn't afford another year of full-time college while starting a new sales territory. While excited about getting recruited by my alma mater, this meeting helped me realize the need of qualified leaders who were willing to sacrifice a good salary for the common good. I did, in fact, believe I could make an impact on the field and in the classroom for years to come. I understood the importance this had on young people to provide that solid foundation needed to be successful.

With all the potential benefits in working in the field of education, I had to evaluate my personal situation. At the time, I was the sole provider and recently purchased a three-bedroom house in the heart of Cordova. Furthermore, Brooke just returned from Alaska, and Beth needed to be home with her for the transition. After a brief discussion with Beth, we decided more income, benefits, and stability in our lives were paramount at that point. We needed a degree of normalcy that included family time.

I told Mr. Chism and Coach Netherland that week I wouldn't take the position and thanked them for the time spent discussing my future. I informed them of my love for Germantown and wanted to continue to help the junior high program if I lived in Shelby County. Both men understood my situation.

One day, while running errands, we were sitting in a lot outside of Target when Beth spoke up, "Get the information you need to make the transition to education and see where it goes. Start to chip away at the license and eventually get into graduate school and finish your master's in education."

"I just cannot pull the trigger with all we have going on. I just need to forget about it. The timing is awful," I replied.

Beth knew somehow this was my destiny and she could see my talent in working with and motivating young people. She always said, "You need to pray and listen to God for your calling because everyone has their spiritual path."

Those words held so much meaning for me for years to come.

As time would march on, I continued to chase the money with Greif Bros. and coach another season at GMS. My territory was expanded to three state areas. My travel was limited to day trips for the most part, working my way out to the edge of my territory and hitting accounts on the way home. Every quarter, I grew my territory with hard work and planning. I found out early I was in a relationship sales role. I found myself entertaining customers more on the weekend and working some events at night.

As my role grew at Greif Bros, the prospect of growing our family was important. As 1992 rolled around, we became pregnant with another child while the middle school season was underway. That season, I declined to work my role as a Friday night coach working the box. My time at home was more valuable than Friday Night Football. As the '92 season started to unfold, my time as a volunteer coach was about to come to a halt. With a young family, pregnant wife, and a new job, something had to give. After much prayer and discussion, I decided to give up my role as a junior high football coach at the conclusion of the season.

That fall, we also received heart-wrenching news that Beth's pregnancy, after several months, had miscarried. This was a difficult time in our young lives. We desperately needed peace and stability through our faith. Beth and I wanted to have more children and that was certainly a priority moving forward. The next year, we continued working toward our goal of stability in our family with the hopes of adding more members in the not-too-distant future.

Our faith life was a driving force in our lives. We wanted to work through Christ to ensure that our family was protected and provided for, keeping an open heart for whatever the future held. In doing this, the Holy Spirit would yet again steer us in a direction that would provide many blessings in the future.

CHAPTER 15

IT'S A GOD THING

BACK IN 1993, a series of life-altering events would eventually set a new course to our young family. First, my position with Greif Bros. was secure with a stable income and benefits. Also, over the past year my territory was growing in revenue, and my customer base had expanded 20 percent from the previous year. With all the success over the past couple years, an opportunity to increase my income and management opportunities presented itself. At that time, my father, Ron, was a successful regional manager with James Hardie Building Products, working out of Dallas as a central regional manager for the company. He had been with Hardie for a couple years, and with his building material expertise, he put this Australian company on the map in the United States. This was due to his sales and distribution history in the Southern Sun Belt states in which Hardie was expanding their customer base.

One day, out of the blue, I asked Dad how business was going, and he explained to me how much success they were having with their fiber cement building product in the Texas region. I inquired about potential positions for hire, and he explained nepotism rules. I could not work in his region, but I potentially could in another part of the country.

Two weeks later, I was granted an interview with the East Coast manager and landed a job as a territory sales representative with James Hardie Building Products. This was now my third sales job in my first four years of employment. I now could make a better annual salary with a commission plan, company car, and better health benefits. Gabe Ferrazzano, the East Coast regional manager, gave me a choice between the Carolina market (North and South Carolina) or the Mid-Atlantic market (Maryland, Pennsylvania, Delaware, and the southern half of New Jersey). Once on board, I had about a week to decide.

Beth and I researched everything we could about both areas, and there were pros and cons to both. Part of the decision-making process was to let God be a part of it. So, we asked Him for His guidance and clarity. We have learned over the years that our prayer life has been extremely important in our ability to make sound decisions.

After five days of research and tons of prayers, we both had clarity before the deadline arrived. It's wild and extremely tough to explain; however, our choice was a city about thirty miles northeast of Baltimore, up interstate 95, called Bel Air, Maryland. The negatives clearly outweighed those of the Carolinas market, which included the cost of living, traffic, state income tax, and weather. Trust me, being married to a Florida girl, the temptation of living in a sunny beach community in Charleston, South Carolina, was thoroughly explored. However, looking back, the Holy Spirit was pulling us to the Mid-Atlantic region. Beth and I thought it would be an opportunity to see another part of the country and experience life beyond the southern states in which we both had lived our entire lives. The decision to go to Bel Air was a flat-out "God thing".

As we began to put our house on the market and pack, we started to get excited about the opportunity to experience life outside of Memphis. At that time, the housing market was solid, and we were able to sell our house in Cordova in the first weekend, surprisingly without a realtor.

Life, once again, was moving fast. Beth and I embraced the change and rolled with it. The first two weeks, until the townhouse was available to move into, we lived in an extended-stay hotel community in Baltimore. In those two weeks, we conceived our second child, Michael. Brooke was approaching five years old and desperately wanted a little brother or sister. Ever since the miscarriage, a void had been in our life. With the instruction of her OB/GYN, we wanted to take some time before we started trying once again.

A couple weeks after we made the drive to our new home in Bel Air, I began hitting the road to get my territory off to a good start. While on the road one night, I received a phone call from Beth that she had tested positive after taking two home pregnancy tests. We were elated, but we were also extremely concerned.

A couple years prior, when Beth had become pregnant, it ended in month seven with a miscarriage; we experienced a difficult situation that could undoubtedly be repeated in the coming months. Beth's pregnancies aren't your typical gestation cycle that most of the women experience. No, not even close.

When Beth was the tender age of twelve, she was at a birthday party at her friend's house when she began to bleed uncontrollably for no apparent reason. Her bleeding was well beyond the typical menstrual cycle that girls her age begin to experience. Beth was rushed to a hospital to figure out the cause of this emergency, and it was determined that Beth, in fact, had a unique situation. It was discovered that she had a double uterus along with two cervixes that made up her female reproductive anatomy. At the time of her uncontrollable bleeding episode, it was also determined that her right cervix was closed and had to be opened surgically to allow flow. Moving forward, she would experience two monthly cycles.

Back in the mid-80s, not a lot of information was known of this condition, and a team of OB/GYN specialists were brought in to perform the surgery. Also, it was disclosed at the time there was a good chance she would never have children later in life; furthermore, important considerations were made to remove one or both uteruses to prevent a pregnancy that could perhaps cause major damage to Beth in the coming years. Her parents were adamant about leaving her body alone and only allowed the surgery to create blood flow to her right cervix. This undoubtedly was a fantastic decision; however, an OB/GYN specialist would have to be up-to-speed in the event of a future pregnancy ever taking place.

Brooke Whitney certainly disproved the theory of Beth not getting pregnant and not being able to bear children. Brooke was born from her left uterus, which happens to be the normal size in her reproductive make-up. The right uterus, on the other hand, is a different story. The right uterus was about a third of the size of a normal uterus. Our last miscarriage involved Beth becoming pregnant in the smaller of the two.

After Beth's news was revealed that she was pregnant, both excitement and anticipation were controlling our emotions. We had the excitement of another child along with the anticipation of a pregnancy that could be, in fact, in the smaller uterus. It was time to find a high-risk OB/GYN who could accommodate Beth's didelphic uterus.

She began by calling her current OB/GYN in Memphis to begin the search of high-risk doctors in the Maryland area. A couple practices were recommended; however, after several interviews with multiple doctors, Beth was still not comfortable in making her final decision. At the height of our frustration, she ran across an article in a magazine talking about a high-risk OB who was doing cutting-edge treatment to aid mothers who were experiencing high-risk medical conditions while pregnant. The article spoke of different methods to help high-risk mothers extend their pregnancy, if possible, in order to get closer to term (forty weeks). He was in the Townson area, thirty miles from Bel Air; however, she was driven to meet him and get his take on her rare condition. His name was Dr. Fred Buchanan.

Her first meeting with Dr. Buchanan was over the phone. He

gathered as much information as possible about her condition and history. Upon hearing Beth's story, she was pushed up the line to see him that week.

Beth and I walked through the foyer of the medical complex toward the elevator when she stopped me in mid-stride. "I have a good feeling about Dr. Buchanan. Let's say a quick prayer for guidance and to confirm this is where we need to be."

After we were called back, we waited for almost an hour in the examination room. *This guy must be highly sought after*, I thought. It was a total zoo in that office. When he finally entered the room, the pleasantries were short, and he quickly went to work.

Dr. Buchanan was to the point and left zero on the table. After her first ultrasound and examination, he explained that her pregnancy was in her smaller uterus once again. Beth began to cry.

"Hang on," he said as he continued to read her chart. "You're not going to believe what I'm about to tell you, but when you had your procedure back in the seventies, I was actually there."

Beth and I were puzzled about what we just heard as our eyes locked in wonder.

"Yes, I was a fellow back in the late '70s and was invited to fly to observe this unusual surgery that was performed by Dr. Phil Meadows in Memphis, Tennessee."

The surgery he was referring to was Beth's procedure to repair and redirect the blood flow coming from one of the blocked cervixes. Beth was no longer crying as he continued to explain, "As matter of fact, your current doctor back home, Ted Smead, and I were roommates at Johns Hopkins. We haven't spoken in a while, but I have a feeling that's going to change soon."

Beth and I were speechless. The odds of obtaining a doctor 1,000 miles from home who was familiar with her case was astonishing.

"That case was one of the first documented and now is published in medical journals," he said.

As the meeting continued, Dr. Buchanan informed Beth once

again of the high-risk nature of her condition and explained the high percentage of miscarriages associated with didelphic uterus. "I will use every technique available to extend your pregnancy, if possible."

As Beth and I sat there listening intensely, I could sense that Beth was eager to hammer him with questions to help her understand.

"Unfortunately, I hate to inform you, but you need to get mentally prepared for a miscarriage or an extreme premature baby because it very well could happen. It's almost like someone having triplets based on the size of your uterus that the fetus is in," he explained in a somber voice.

There was a pause in his explanation and that's when she jumped into the conversation. The moment she heard the word "miscarriage," Beth decided to take the reins.

"Dr. Buchanan" she said with an authoritative voice. "I appreciate you being straight forward, transparent, and honest. I love the fact that you have seen my case firsthand, and that you were roommates with my terrific doctor back in Memphis, who delivered my first child. In saying this, I want you to know you are going to get me as close to term as possible, and a miscarriage is out of the question. Dr. Buchanan, I found you through the grace of God and through prayer, and I will do whatever it takes to get as close to our due date as possible."

Frankly, I couldn't believe what I was hearing. She flat out told him: "We are having this baby, so bring your A game!"

After a brief pause, Dr. Buchanan said, "I will do everything in my power to get your baby here healthy."

The pregnancy started normal, but we anticipated things could happen or change in a hurry. We decided to start a fifty-four-day novena that included twenty-seven days of petition and twenty-seven days of thanksgiving. This petition is known as the Miraculous 54-Day Rosary Novena. At the time, I had not converted to Catholicism, but I followed Beth's lead. Beth understood that, along with an excellent doctor and with medical breakthroughs, our spiritual life needed a boost to bring our new healthy baby into our world.

While we were preparing for an intense pregnancy, I was still getting started in my new territory with a ton of work ahead in the coming months to grow my customer base in order to hit big numbers in the coming year. Our plan was set.

A couple months went by, and Beth set up a weekly checkup to ensure everything was progressing nicely. However, at seventeen weeks, Beth started to experience minor bleeding and severe pains in her abdomen that warranted an unscheduled visit to the doctor's office to find out that Beth was, in fact, going into preterm labor. He quickly reminded us to be prepared for the fact we may not to go to term, and the chances of a miscarriage were high. He then went on to explain and remind us of how it's like having triplets in a very small area.

She then quickly reminded him of holding up his end of the bargain. "Doc, get me close to forty weeks no matter what as we *are not* losing this baby!"

That afternoon, when we returned home, the reality of the situation grew heavy. As we learned from the visit, she was seventeen weeks pregnant and already 2 cm dilated. We also discovered that our baby was a boy. Beth's instructions were to begin bedrest and remain as still as much as possible. Furthermore, the only time she was to stand up and walk was to use the bathroom. We then contacted out-of-state family members to come up and rotate a schedule that would allow me to work my territory. My mom agreed to come in from Dallas in a few days to begin living with us. In the meantime, Dr. Buchanan put Beth on a terbutaline pump. This medicine is used only to slow the contractions down to prevent labor from occurring. She was then coached by Dr. Buchanan's team on how to monitor the contractions using a device that would count the contractions. Then she would send the information over a landline to determine if she needed another hit of the terbutaline. She had to inject a needle into her own hip when needed (as she didn't trust me to do it!).

Beth, being a cradle Catholic, had taken a couple trips to Medjugorje in the former Yugoslavia and has seen miracles with her own eyes. Her spiritual connection with God and the Holy Spirit were truly remarkable, and she had witnessed firsthand the power of prayer. The fifty-four-day novena included praying the rosary and asking God through his mother Mary for a healthy baby boy. During the last twenty-seven days of the novena, we would thank God, praying through Mary and other saints, for our blessing in making our way through the pregnancy and for our young family. You must pray every day, without skipping one, or it reverts to the beginning. It's truly a discipline of prayer and an incredible way to connect with the Holy Spirit. At the time, I was officially Episcopalian, but I had gone to Catholic mass ever since Beth and I met, so this novena period gave me an opportunity to learn more about Catholicism. My prayer life continued to be blessed.

As we approached thirty weeks, the contractions increased dramatically. At twenty-eight weeks, Beth's checkup was not so good. Her contractions were becoming more repetitive, and we found out she was 3 cm dilated. Dr. Buchanan informed us we needed to go to Greater Baltimore Medical Center (GBMC) immediately and prepare for anything. He then told her that she would be put on magnesium sulfate. He explained that magnesium would shut down any involuntary muscular contractions for a twenty-four-hour period and hopefully would help her body reset to decline her uterine activity and get her to week thirty at the very minimum.

As we made it to the hospital, Beth was immediately put on the magnesium sulfate in the ICU ward so that every vital could be monitored for her safety. The moment the treatment began, I was warned by nurses she would become delirious and have a tough time speaking, and to not let her drink anything. She was allowed ice chips once per hour. They warned me that this twenty-four-hour period would be rough, and she would be extremely thirsty and groggy. Man, they weren't kidding. After she was lifted from the magnesium, a sense of relief was immediate. It seemed that the technique worked; it shut down all contractions, and she was able to readminister the pump when her contractions started again. It wasn't a question of if, it was a question of when they would start again. The hope was that she could begin using the pump once again to get her to term. But in the meantime, she needed to spend the next three weeks at GBMC to be constantly monitored. While at the hospital, we went to the NICU with the possibility of baby Michael spending some time in it.

Beth's fortitude and mental toughness were remarkable while enduring through those uncharted waters. Whenever I shared those sentiments with her, she would always say, "It's not me; it's God. God gets all the glory!"

Upon returning home, we were now in week thirty-two and were thrilled that we made it this far. However, we were desperate for more. Every hour, day, or week was needed for our baby. The longer the better. Our tour of the NICU was sobering and surreal, and we realized a few more weeks would go a long way.

In the thirty-fourth week, we were back at GBMC for another round of magnesium sulfate. It was the same procedure, but this time they released us after three days. Once again, the pump was back at work. Dr. Buchanan was so amazing in his planning and coaching, and we were willing to do whatever it took to make this a success. The original due date was January 21, and now we were five weeks shy of that date. Dr. Buchanan said we were home free, but any more time is icing on the cake. Beth and I agreed more icing was needed.

In the early afternoon on Friday, December 21, while on the phone in my basement office, Miles came downstairs and announced in a mild tone: "It might be time."

"Time for what?" I asked as I interrupted my boss mid-conversation.

"The baby," he replied.

"Oh. I've need to go, Gabe," I said as I hung up the phone before hearing a response. I then shot up the stairs like a cannonball and started to grab prepacked bags and supplies.

"This is not a drill, Mike. My water just broke," she said.

I must have been going 90 mph on I-95 south for that thirty-five-minute drive to Baltimore. It was imperative we make it to GBMC because of the advanced NICU this hospital had to offer. We called ahead to provide the team a heads-up.

By the time we arrived, her pain level had increased dramatically, and she was admitted immediately. By this time, almost the entire floor knew our name because of the multiple trips and how unusual her situation was. The entire team was accounted for and ready, except for one person: Dr. Fred Buchanan. He was stuck in bumper-to-bumper traffic at the height of rush hour.

As her team, prepared an IV and checked her dilation, her pain was unbearable. "I'm hurting! I'm hurting!" Beth yelled at the top of her lungs. A nurse nervously walked in. "I'm having this baby now!"

By this time, our baby was crowning as she grew to eight centimeters. "Don't push, Mrs. O'Neill. I will get the doctor who is on call," the nurse said as Dr. Buchanan came walking briskly through the door.

"Okay, everyone. We are having this baby right now. No epidural or pain meds," he said as he rolled up his sleeves and put his surgical gloves on. "Push, Beth!"

Within ten minutes, our sweet baby boy, Ronald Michael O'Neill III, officially joined the party, weighing 5.12 oz, exactly one month short of his intended due date. What a miraculous day!

Through this entire process, my faith and love only grew deeper for God. My wife showed me her spirit and was an incredible witness to her faith. Years later, I would go through the RCIA program to convert to Catholicism. Having our son accelerated my commitment to this process, and it taught me how God has played such an important role in our marriage and family, and now in my fight against cancer.

God has extended my life and has provided strength to battle this awful disease. I truly believe that this experience began a deeper relationship with the Holy Spirit, and I will call on God's help and guidance in many aspects of my life. I'm genuinely blessed by His salvation and count my blessings every day. The sacrament of marriage and family is a true blessing, and it's part of God's plan.

"It's a God thing!"

CHAPTER 16

THE TEMPTATION IS REAL

AFTER MICHAEL WAS born and my mom and sister Liz returned to Dallas, life was starting to return to normal. Unfortunately, it was the dead of winter in Maryland, and Beth and I calculated around seventeen snow/ice storms, including two major nor'easters that caused a major loss of power and cost billions of dollars. We had never experienced anything remotely like that before. Even people across the Mid-Atlantic were talking about how brutal the winter was. I remember the first couple of snow falls were beautiful, then after the tenth one, we were begging for the Memphis heat and humidity.

As I returned to my territory after the birth of Michael at the Christmas holidays, I began to travel once again. For that period while Beth was pregnant with Michael, I refused to do any overnight stays. I threw myself back into my territory with working trade shows, calling on builders and architects, and doing anything and everything possible to pull this unique fiber cement through the buying channel. This territory was brand new to Hardie and a tough market to penetrate because there was not a big hardboard siding market.

My numbers were solid, but my competitive makeup was driving me to do more. I hit lumberyards from Ocean City, Maryland, to the Poconos, to the Jersey Shore. I was working builder shows and training lumberyard sales reps on the features and benefits of this incredible product. As spring hit, I began to make sales calls in Pennsylvania from Philly to Pittsburgh and points in between.

As I made my way around my territory, I really embraced the opportunity to meet new people and work in a part of the country with so much to offer. I also enjoyed seeing a product so unique that also had such a great history behind it.

Just as I began to open my territory up, Hardie decided to hire another sales rep who would aid in opening the Ohio and West Virginia market, but it also included the Western Pennsylvania/New York territories, which included Pittsburg. Early on, my regional manager told me this day would come and instructed me to get Pittsburgh off the ground. The Mid-Atlantic had its challenges, but we were making some progress, and overall enjoyed my job with James Hardie.

On one of my business trips in February 1994, Beth decided to take our little ones to Collierville to visit her parents. Michael, who was just over two months old, had a lingering cold for about a month, and Beth wanted to take him to Memphis to get checked out by a long-time family pediatrician. He was having difficulty breathing, and after one incident in Bel Air, we had to call 911 because he had turned blue due to lack of oxygen. Because he was born four weeks early, we were always on guard. It turned out to be the passing of a mucus plug, but it sure got our attention. He was not even six pounds and continued to struggle after multiple doctor visits. After Beth made the trip down South, the next morning, Michael was taken to the pediatrician's office in Collierville. Beth has that innate ability to determine when something was medically wrong with our children, and she wanted some answers.

Upon arriving at the doctor's appointment in Collierville, as Michael was being evaluated, he began to turn blue and struggled to breathe. The physician immediately called for an ambulance to be transported to LeBonheur Children's Hospital in downtown Memphis. Hours later, it was discovered Michael had a terrible case of RSV, a respiratory virus that can affect and hospitalize infants very early in life. The virus especially affects infants under one year old in the winter months. Little Michael fit both of those criteria in his early life. On their way to the hospital, I received a phone call that they were being transported to LeBonheur and Michael was having major difficulties breathing. My heart sank.

"What is going on? Where are you now? What's the doctor saying?"

I could barely hear because of the sound of the ambulance. Beth said she would call me back once they arrived at LeBonheur. At the time of the phone call, I was working a trade show in Philadelphia, Pennsylvania, over a thousand miles away and immediately began looking for flights out of Philly, Baltimore, and D.C. with zero luck. All flights were booked, and the airport in Philadelphia was shut down due to ice. Within an hour, I was checked out and headed back to Bel Air, Maryland, for more clothes and items Beth wanted me to pick up. After a quick stop, I was on the way to Memphis.

As I made my way into Virginia, the freezing rain began to fall. It took almost two and a half days of straight driving to make it to the hospital. Again, this is before cell phones had saturated our society. I would stop to get updates or pull over when my beeper went off. The closer I got to Memphis, the more intense the storm was. It took me eight hours to make it from Nashville to Memphis to complete the last leg of the trip.

However, through many prayers and careful driving, I made it to the ICU at LeBonheur Children's Hospital in downtown Memphis. Upon arrival, I learned that baby Michael was doing a little better with breathing treatments on the hour. Poor Beth was exhausted. These might have been the longest and most intense days in our young marriage. I distinctly remember sitting in the hospital room looking out and seeing huge limbs snapping off trees constantly, day and night. You could hear the cracking from five floors up. With God's blessing, we were in the right place. The entire region went without power for several weeks; however, the hospital never lost power because of their backup system. The doctors and staff took incredible care of Michael, but his bout with RSV lasted another three to four months. This was a terrible time, but God blessed our family once again.

The moment things settled down and Michael was improving, we made it back to Maryland and survived our first Mid-Atlantic winter. Spring was around the corner, and it couldn't arrive fast enough.

By March, I was knee-deep back in the territory calling on potential customers and working trade shows on the weekends. My regional manager also wanted me to train the new sales rep, Ralph DiMartino, for the Pittsburgh market. Bi-monthly, I went to western Pennsylvania to work with Ralph. In the process, we became good friends.

It was August, and Ralph called me the weekend before our last training session would take place. "Okay, Mike. Next weekend I have tickets to the Pitt/Texas game on Saturday and the Steelers/Cowboys game on Sunday! What do you think? You're a Cowboys fan, and I want to thank you for working with me over the last few months."

"Really? I need to clear it with Beth, but it sounds great!"

My sweet wife, knowing my love for the game and leaving it cold turkey a couple years ago, gave me the green light to overdose on some football that weekend.

The weather that weekend was close to perfect, and Ralph had everything ready. On Saturday, the Pitt/Texas game went down to the wire in a shoot-out with Texas winning in the final minute. The rest of the afternoon we gorged on Italian food and watched hours of college football at a sports pub right next to his downtown apartment.

That Sunday morning, before we left for Three Rivers Stadium, Ralph and I were watching one of the earlier games before we joined the tailgate at the stadium. During one of the games we were watching,

I asked Ralph if he understood why this team was running cover two and why the other team failed to adjust their routes train to beat the coverage. He looked at me like I was talking another language.

I told him, "If the offense would run cover two beater with a corner route, that would force the defense to get on their heels. Usually, a slot receiver will take off straight down the field at forty-five degrees toward the corner. It's called a corner route or cover two beater. This will put him beyond the rolled-up corner that's playing the flats, and the safety will struggle to cover the deep corner behind him. Every coverage has its weakness. In cover two, it's the four vertical routes that will force the defense to change their tactics. I can't believe they are not picking up on that."

Ralph sat there and still said nothing. About then, the NBC commentator broke down cover two and described how the corner route could provide a huge play for the offense if they picked up on it. The commentator broke it down pretty much as I described it to Ralph in his living room.

"Damn, Mike, why aren't you coaching football?" Ralph asked.

To that point, I never mentioned once to Ralph that I ever coached or considered pursuing it as a profession. He then told me, "I just watch the QB get the snap and follow the ball until the play is over. What are you watching?"

Suddenly, the light switch was turned on once again. The sudden passion of the game and everything that I loved about it was overwhelming. I kept those thoughts and feelings to myself for the rest of the weekend.

On the way home to Baltimore later that evening, I couldn't get the thought of coaching football out of my head. Why was I not pursing my passion? Were Coach Netherland and Principal Chism right? Beth would ask me every fall if I missed it all and if I ever had second thoughts about my temptation to pursue my dream. Every time I would answer no because business and sales would bring in more money and this is what I needed to do for our family. However, after a month went by after that football weekend in Pittsburgh, I constantly thought about obtaining my master's degree to begin my career as a teacher/coach. I enjoyed my position at James Hardie, but my calling was elsewhere. Truly, the major factors motivating me in my business career were making money and obtaining better perks. I had bounced around three companies in three different industries and felt like there was more for me to do in my life than just closing deals. My early coaching experience had opened my eyes and kindled my passion to coach, and now I was hungry for more. That football weekend in Pittsburgh only rekindled the fire burning inside me.

CHAPTER 17

HOW BAD DO YOU WANT IT?

WHEN RETURNING HOME from Pittsburgh that Sunday, the five-hour drive gave me some time to dissect and reflect on the football weekend and if, in fact, I wanted to entertain the possibility to make a career jump. It's one thing to make a career move if you are in the same industry or line of work; however, diving into a completely different occupation requires passion and commitment, especially when that line of work only offers half the salary and benefits than you are currently making. There were so many thoughts going through my head that weekend and the biggest one was this: *Can I put my family on this potentially difficult road ahead? Is it fair to Beth and the children to jump careers to pursue my true passion and perhaps my spiritual gifts?*

I only wish I would have asked Dr. Setterlund more questions back when I was being recruited by Germantown to make the switch. Furthermore, a couple years had passed and I wondered if the master's requirements been altered.

As I approached Bel Air, the curiosity and passion to gear up for a career change to education was almost downright overwhelming. As I strongly began to feel my passion to coach, once again I promised myself, I would not even entertain the prospect without Beth's complete backing or if she had any doubt about a possible transition to another career. I was not going to apply any undue pressure, but I simply wanted to have a conversation about what I was currently feeling.

That Sunday night when I returned, Beth and I had an extensive and thorough conversation about what happened in Pittsburgh. As we began talking, I could feel her sense of excitement about me following my dream. Beth's unselfish attitude about pursuing life goals were put on the front burner. Beth was extremely supportive and wanted to take the next week to research the exact process and how long it would take to make the transition. We would look at personal finances and determine how much school she had left to finish also. This plan would have several moving parts, but the most important item now in planning to execute was gathering information. Once we obtained what exactly was needed to accomplish my goal of education, a more formalized plan would be put in place.

That week I got to work. I reached out to the University of Memphis to formally examine my undergrad transcripts to determine what was needed to qualify for the graduate program at Memphis. The admissions department explained that a couple electives were needed to go along with the business management degree to qualify for graduate school.

By that time, Beth had made her way down armed with a yellow legal pad and pen. "Hey. Let's talk timelines and goals."

"Just got off the phone with Memphis, and they explained what classes I need to take to get in the master's program. I can enroll in the Hartford Community College up the road and wrap those up while I'm working the territory the next few months. Next, I need to pass the Miller Analogies Test to even be considered for graduate school at the University of Memphis," I said as she frantically wrote every word down.

"I've been thinking about finishing up my degree too," she said. "I need eighteen hours, and I can live with my parents while you're up here wrapping things up. If you're going to be a teacher, I need to jump in the workforce at some point."

Beth and I continued to update our timeline as information was obtained. After our week of intense planning, I enrolled at a community college in Bel Air, and Beth did the same in Memphis. Life once again was moving extremely fast. The next week we loaded up for Memphis to convoy home to make the move to her parents' house, and I successfully completed hurdle one by passing the MAT entrance exam that Saturday. We both realized that this period would be the toughest to execute to make this happen for two reasons. First, Beth going back to school to take a full eighteen hours with two children alone, and second, the time we would spend away from each other and the children. We both understood the sacrifice and commitment to make this happen would have its challenges. We also understood that I was not getting any younger and the time to make this happen was now!

By the middle of September, both Beth and I were back in college. The biggest issue was being one thousand miles away from one another, getting those prerequisite classes behind me while working at James Hardie, and with Beth wrapping up her degree. That was the plan that fall. Meanwhile, I continued to work hard to get this territory off the ground. I knew in a few months I would make my way back to Memphis, but I wanted to leave on a great note. As the semester ended, I gave Hardie my two-week notice, but I knew the hardest part was informing my dad of my plans to leave his company and start my master's to begin a life in education/coaching.

Unfortunately, it went about how I thought it would: not well. I called on a Monday morning. This was an ambush, and I really couldn't expect him to fully understand at that time. He picked up on the first ring. "Ron O'Neill."

"Dad, it's Mike."

"Hey, Mike. How are things in Baltimore? Have a good weekend? Beth and the kids doing well?"

As the barrage of questions came in, my only answers were "yes, sir" and "good."

I cut to the chase. "Dad, I've decided I'm leaving James Hardie to pursue my dream of coaching high school football."

After a bit of time for it to sink in, he responded, "Mike, I think you're being short-sighted by not giving enough time to settle in the new territory. I'm very disappointed in hearing this news."

He was extremely surprised because he was getting great reports regarding my work ethic, and things were starting to happen.

"Mike, you need to consider the lifestyle you would be settling for based on the income potential as a high school teacher/coach. Beth will have to work," he reminded me.

"Dad, you're right. These are things I have struggled with for the past few years. I need to give it a shot because I'm being pushed in that direction somehow. I know that's hard to understand, but I need to pursue education at this stage of my life."

It was a tough conversation, and it would take a couple of years before he understood my true ambition and reasons for getting into this profession.

After three extremely long months living in Bel Air alone, I moved to Collierville to join my family. The plan was taking shape. Beth knocked out a full load to graduate college that December. While in Maryland, I completed my prerequisites to successfully start the master's program and eventually picked up a job working twelve-hour shifts at a local medical waste facility near downtown Memphis while taking the first semester of classes that spring.

After six months at the medical waste facility, I knew I had to find another gig. By then, I figured out the remote chance of picking up a virus or something far worse could happen. Over that six-month period, I had to get multiple hepatitis shots and be extremely careful not to get stuck with discarded needles or other medical waste.

One night, with an hour left in my shift, I was working on the incineration line attempting to clean my area of waste before the graveyard shift began. As I was grabbing chipboard containers and corrugated boxes to discard them into the furnace, I noticed a box that had fallen off the conveyor belt and landed on its side. I bent down to pick it up. "What!" I yelled as I stared at a human hand that somehow found its way out of the container.

It was clearly time to shift gears for both my health and the health of everyone in my family, and I quickly found another job while I continued to work to achieve my goals.

As we continued our unconventional and extremely busy transition to get to the destination Beth and I set forth, we became pregnant with our third child, Mary Elizabeth. We were thrilled but also understood there could be obvious complications based on Beth's unique medical makeup. After a visit to her OB/GYN, it was announced that she was once again pregnant in her smaller uterus.

For now, we continued to endure my fall work/school schedule and Beth's new job as a manager. As the spring semester ended, some important decisions had to be made about the current path we were on. With the likelihood of bedrest and uncertainty, we came to the realization that I needed to scrap the course I was on and get back to the business world.

It took a few weeks, but I landed a job back in the industrial packaging industry with Willamette Corporation as a corrugated box manufacturer territory rep in the Memphis area. I was back in the game. The upside was it required zero overnight travel outside of an occasional training or sales convention, and it came with a company car and full benefits. By this time, I understood there was a better than good chance that the coaching dream was coming to a screeching halt.

Just like clockwork, Beth went to bedrest around four and a half months into her pregnancy with Mary as I began my training with the new company. Thankfully, this pregnancy went much smoother than the last one. Praise the Lord! I guess little Mike paved the way for his little sister. There was no terbutaline pump or magnesium sulfate this time, and she almost made it to term when she began to feel contractions. Unfortunately, the most difficult part for her was after the birth of Mary, when she required surgery to stop the bleeding. She was hemorrhaging and lost major blood that required an emergency hysterectomy, which was 100 percent successful. September 6, 1995 was a glorious day with the birth of our third child, Mary Elizabeth O'Neill. She was so perfect and beautiful. However, later that night, while Beth was recovering from a long and emotional day, we sadly realized we would not have any more children. However, as the night almost turned to morning, we understood how blessed we were to have three of the best and most perfect children anyone could ever imagine. God is great!

CHAPTER 18

THE ACCORDION TECHNIQUE

A FULL YEAR WENT by. I received a call from a good friend, Jean Paul Gentleman. He told me how much money was in the heavy equipment industry as an outside sales rep and what a great time he had doing it. He quickly got my attention and set me up with an interview to possibly take over the North Shelby County territory. The company was United Equipment, and they were the sole CASE Construction dealership that covered a 150-mile radius of Memphis. Even though the job was, for the most part, a commission job with a monthly draw, I liked the idea that United had exclusive rights to sales in their assigned territory with CASE and an assortment of other products. Since the economy and building were both in a major growth mode, it seemed appropriate to jump ship again. This time it came with unlimited earnings potential.

Overall, my last job in the heavy equipment industry was my favorite. My latest sales job of hustling heavy construction equipment was probably the most rewarding in terms of business. For starters, my company truck was an F-350. A diesel truck that sounded like an airplane when I pulled into the neighborhood. Also, the dress code was much more relaxed—blue jeans, golf shirts, and steel-toed boots. I was on the job site or trailers constantly, and the last thing foreman and construction workers want to see are neckties and khakis. Next, I sold excavators, bulldozers, and backhoes, just to name a few.

My four-year-old son thought I was a superhero. Every time I would load up a backhoe or skid-steer for an early morning product demo, that evening I would take it home and occasionally back it off the trailer and give young Mike a spin. I could have been a major league baseball player or an NFL head coach, but I had the feeling little Michael liked this way better.

As I started my third year at United, I continued to grow my territory, and the money was fantastic. There were a few signs that the economy was slowing nationwide, but not in Shelby County. Even though we were a small to medium-sized business, my coworkers were my good friends; they were some of the best and most professional businesspeople I have ever been around.

In the meantime, Beth was becoming quite the salesperson herself. Hands down better than me. She was in telecom and a master at building relationships and trust with her customers. She has won numerous awards and attended several President Clubs for her outstanding performance.

As Beth and I were sinking our teeth into our careers, Beth had really started making a name for herself. After she got on board with CompuServe, she experienced several corporate buyouts, but she was always retained because of her outstanding role as a world-class salesperson. Her customers simply loved her because she always fought for them internally. She was fantastic in making the customer feel like they were vested and part of the process in every deal she packaged.

I was enjoying my time at United Equipment, and my territory had gained ample numbers over the past four years. However, the economy was cooling a bit, but my sales were still strong. One spring weekend, the Ducks Unlimited Company requested our United Equipment to donate and use some of our equipment to build their tracks for their four-wheelers and off-road vehicles to demonstrate their product capabilities. In exchange, they allowed us to set up a booth (at no charge) to hand out information of our product line. I had a ton of customers and prospects who were outdoorsmen, and I figured the exposure wouldn't hurt. The show was in my territory, so I set up and worked the United Equipment booth on a beautiful, warm Saturday. It turned out to be a good show that produced several sales leads. As the afternoon began to wind down, I noticed a booth across from mine promoting a giveaway. Ducks Unlimited was promoting their services while giving away a Suzuki Grand Vitara in a free raffle.

As I started to pack up my booth and call it a week, I went over to their tent and filled out the required information for the drawing that would be done at the end of business that day. I went to the booth, filled out one free drawing card, folded it the way Beth does when she enters drawings, and put it in the box. We called it "the accordion technique." Ducks Unlimited would announce the winner the next day when the show wrapped up early afternoon on Sunday. As I lugged my gear to my truck, I called Beth to tell her I was on the way home and informed her that I entered a drawing.

"Yes, yes. I folded it the way you do," I insisted.

Let me share the secret of folding a raffle ticket back in the '90s. With today's digital capabilities, this technique is completely useless, but I will share it anyway. The technique is simple. You kind of fold it like an accordion. Yes, fold it in small segments as many times as possible until it looks like an accordion. Beth swears by it! She says when the person is fishing the winning ticket out of the box, it has extra volume to attract the attention and provides a better chance to get pulled. Makes sense, I guess. It never worked for me before because I rarely bothered to enter these types of contests.

The next morning, we went to mass followed by a nice lunch and was home around one p.m. The plan for the day was a quick change of clothes and catch up on some yard work. Beth was upstairs in her office to check on something. Not long after, she started to yell at the top of her lungs, "You won! You won!"

The sound I heard was somewhat muffled because I was downstairs about to walk out of the garage door to start some yardwork. At first, by the volume of her voice, I thought something was wrong and did an about face and quickly walked toward the stairs. The closer I got, the louder it was because Beth was coming down, then going up, then down, then up the stairs, yelling, "You won! You won!"

"I won what?" I yelled back.

"You won the car that you signed up for yesterday at the Ducks Unlimited show!"

I completely forgot I entered a drawing. "Beth, Beth, slow down!"

As she stopped at the midway point on the stairs, hanging on the banister, almost out of breath, I said, "Beth, it's probably some marketing bologna that wants you to test drive the Suzuki."

At that point, she looked me dead in the eye and said, "Why would they call you on a Sunday morning? The message was from two hours ago! No one markets on Sunday mornings!"

She had a point. Just like that, we both took off in a sprint back upstairs to her office to listen to the message once again.

"This is (so-and-so) from Ducks Unlimited, and we are trying to get ahold of Mike O'Neill from Collierville to inform him that he is the winner of the Suzuki Grand Vitara that was drawn this morning."

"See? I told you!" Beth said.

Within five minutes, the entire family was back in the car racing down Poplar Avenue to head to Ducks Unlimited where the event was taking place. As we unloaded, the entire family beelined to the Ducks Unlimited tent where I filled out the potential winning ticket. I was thinking that this was too good to be true. When I arrived at the table, I simply asked the young lady who was currently working the booth if a winner had been drawn for the raffle. She quickly stated without any emotion, "Yes, some guy named Mike from Collierville."

It had to sink in for a second. Then, I started acting like Beth did about thirty minutes ago when she was racing up and down the stairs yelling that I won a car. "I'm Mike! I'm Mike from Collierville. I'm your winner."

I dug in my back pocket to shovel out my driver's license as quickly as possible while my heart rate was probably topping 200 bpm.

By midweek, we were instructed to go by the dealership and collect our prize. To my surprise, the process took much longer than simply driving a newly won car off the lot. For starters, I had to write a check for the sales tax for the prize I had just won. Before I could call this car my own, I had to pay about $1,700 out of the gate to cover the sales tax. The latest unexpected cost helped me make up my mind on what to do with the new vehicle. Time to sell.

Later that week as life bounced back to normal, I was back in my territory hitting it as hard as ever. As the day started to wrap up, I began to think again about the proceeds from the sale of the car ($14,000) that was just added to our savings account. It was apparent that I needed to take this money and invest it for solid returns in the next few years. There were so many options to choose. What if I used that money to finish school? As I drove home, I made up my mind to run it by Beth. If she had any resistance or hesitation, I was going to abort the mission completely and never bring it up again. Period.

When I pulled up in the driveway, I saw Beth outside, watering the flowers we planted the day before. After a quick kiss, she said, "What? Do you have something to say?"

"Beth, I've been thinking on how I want to spend that prize money. I believe we have enough so I can wrap up school and then student teach. What do you think?"

"Yes, let's do it! I have been thinking the same thing, but I wanted you to initiate the conversation first. If you did that, I knew your passion to teach and coach was still alive. I'm on board! Let's wrap it up and start your career in education."

I started to cry.

CHAPTER 19

JUMP IN WITH BOTH FEET

I SPENT THE NEXT two weeks confirming that the University of Memphis would accept my hours and asking what exactly was needed to move forward. I began to get excited about my next career. Basically, I had to take a research course and spend an entire summer working and defending a thesis on collaborative learning, as well as my job at United and keep my territory up. I also gave them ample time to find another rep when I stepped away in August of 2001. Leading up to that point, Beth and I made the financial arrangements so I could begin to student teach and coach that fall. The master's program required me to student teach in two different locations in one semester to wrap up my master's degree in December of 2001.

That summer, I began to network and inquire about different locations to coach. At that time, I thought Memphis would assign my schools to student teach and I would seek out a football program to help with after class was out for the day. I didn't need to be at the same school I was performing my student teaching either.

One Sunday, I saw an old friend coming into the church parking lot after the 10:30 service. "Hey, Kevin. How are you?" I asked as we shook hands.

"Great, Mike, it's been a long time. How's everything?" Kevin responded.

As the mass of people were heading to their cars for Sunday lunch, Kevin and I continued to catch up, and I informed him of my current career switch. I had known Kevin since grade school, and he was the current head football coach at Christian Brothers High School in the east Memphis area. It was my father's alma mater, and they had a great football tradition.

"That's right. I can begin student teaching in the fall, and I hope to coach also."

"Mike, your timing is perfect. If you don't mind, I will talk with our administrators to see if we can accommodate your student teaching requirements. This could be a win-win because I need some help this fall. I believe we can make this happen," Kevin confidently insisted.

Unreal, I thought. If Memphis would agree to it, I could student teach the first rotation during football season; that would be almost perfect for my busy schedule that fall. I thanked Kevin for the surprise visit, and he informed me that we would talk early that week.

That Monday, I made some phone calls of my own and reached out to the placement office at the University of Memphis. To my delight, they informed me I could student teach at Christian Brothers High School for the first nine weeks of my student teaching requirement. By midweek, Kevin called me back with the news that CBHS gave me a thumbs-up, pending a drug test and one interview with the head of the business department. By Thursday of that week, my plans to student teach and coach at CBHS were solid. The Brothers seemed excited about me being a part of their community in the coming fall. Kevin explained that having a student teacher was an extremely rare phenomenon, and the timing was perfect because his varsity staff had only three members coaching at the time, and I would be the fourth. I was extremely excited and could hardly wait to begin.

The heavy equipment business started to cool off after an excellent market boom in the mid to late '90s. Housing started to slow and commercial projects were doing about the same. I worked through the month of July and gave my notice at the end of the month. Graciously, United Equipment was extremely supportive of my decision and wasn't completely shocked at my intentions. My friends who worked there knew my story and my ambition to get into education at some point. I was granted permission to leave at any point that was suitable for me to do so. I was very grateful for them hiring me and really enjoyed the experience of life as an outside construction equipment sales representative.

For multiple reasons, I knew it was important to pursue my business career early on for the needs of our family and was so grateful to do so. I'm 100 percent sure that we were meant to spend the time in Maryland to have our son Michael. Then, the Holy Spirit guided us back to eventually seek my inner calling. I am extremely blessed and wouldn't change my path at all.

As the season began, getting used to the grind was nearly impossible, but working to accommodate the grind from a family perspective usually fell on the shoulders of Beth. She received a good taste of it during the two-a-day camp.

"Dang, honey. Are these your new work hours? You've been gone since five a.m., and I haven't seen you until ten p.m. What gives?"

I knew the commitment and hours in football camp would lay that foundation to a successful season. As time passed, she began to understand the work and time needed to get the boys going in the same direction; however, I'm not quite sure if she was able to get used to it.

School began the third week of August, and my class schedule included the business fields of accounting, marketing, and business management. Overall, I sat in or taught six classes. The student teaching plan included the first two six-week grading periods at Christian Brothers and one six-week rotation at Ridgeway High School in Memphis. After I was observed and passed my requirements, I would obtain my teacher license and my master's degree in December 2001. In the meantime, I would coach only at CBHS for the remainder of the season, hopefully through a state championship.

On the coaching front, the staff was as busy as ever and off to an excellent start. Our first contest was the inaugural Bridge Builders Football Classic to kick off the high school 2001 football season. This game was played week zero at the Liberty Bowl Memorial Stadium. The concept was simple and successful: Have two inner city school teams take on two private school programs to get the high school season into full swing.

I clearly remember standing in the tunnel at the Liberty Bowl Memorial Stadium as the Purple Wave was introduced. The anticipation of making my career switch a reality was about to happen. The sight of 10,000 people, accompanied by the sound of the two bands, had my senses in overdrive as we ran to the sidelines. Furthermore, the hard work and buildup to the season opener was epic, and the players and staff were hyped.

The fall of 2001 was impactful on a personal, career, and societal front also. Our lives were as busy as ever. Beth's new career at Sprint Corporation became extremely successful early on in her climb as a businessperson. She was knee-deep into training and establishing a rapport with Memphis's largest employer. The kids' schedules were magnificently organized on a family calendar with every event, game, business trip, and birthday on it. Beth believed "we wing nothing!"

From a societal perspective, 9/11 happened that fall of 2001, and I often think about all the changes and attitudes that came with it. I was giving a business lesson in Coach Luckett's room, when I heard a faint knock. It was Dr. Gossett, and he was bidding for my attention to inform about something as I moved to open door.

"Hey, Dr. Gossett? How can I help you?" I cheerfully asked.

I quickly saw the look of concern on his face.

"Hey, coach. Turn on your TV. A plane just hit the World Trade Center in New York." Without a word, I walked over and turned on the classroom TV and angled it toward thirty students who were sitting quietly in their seats.

That moment will never be forgotten, and it confirmed that I needed to continue working with young people moving forward. I knew life as we knew it would change forever. As far as being a teacher and coach goes, getting back to business was paramount, and we played that next Friday night vs. Evangelical Christian School. One thing we did as a staff that I won't forget is that we never made a reference to our football players of going to war prior to a game. The statement of going to war or battle had a different meaning now. We understood that war was now taking place against terrorism. Many lives were going to be lost. Football was simply a game and yet extremely competitive, but lives were not at stake.

When the third six-week session began, I was relocated a few miles down the road from CBHS to Ridgeway High School. From Collierville, it was about twenty-five minutes away. Then after school, it was on to CBHS for football practice. That was a quick ten-minute drive. After a successful third six weeks of student teaching, I achieved my teacher's certification and master's. That December I was hired by Christian Brothers High School to begin full time in the spring as a business teacher and football coach.

CHAPTER 20

NEW MILLENNIUM, NEW CHALLENGES

THE NEW MILLENNIUM for me was extremely exciting and offered the opportunity to begin the dream of being a high school football coach and classroom business teacher. This decade started our version of Friday Night Football in the O'Neill family. One thing was crystal clear: From late July until November, our lives were busy during the "grind" and would affect every family member in different ways. The grind I'm referring to is simply football season and everything that comes with it.

Without any doubt, the grind was the toughest on the coach's wife. Beth already had a demanding job with a client base that required her to be on call 24/7, not to mention she was a football widow and single parent during those months. The off-season/summer provided some relief, but even out of season, the education/sports life was extremely demanding and time-consuming. The grind, from her perspective, included public criticism of game results and sometimes personal attacks on her husband.

Also, weekends after a Friday night revolved around a win or loss to determine how Saturday and Sunday would play out. A win usually meant an upbeat preparation. A loss was not good. A loss meant a loss of sleep and extra film review starting on Friday almost immediately after the game to figure out the issues. The Saturday after the loss meant developing a plan to correct those mistakes and then start watching film for the opponent next week. Sunday, win or lose, the kids would come in for personal game grades provided by their position coaches, and the mood was determined 100 percent from Friday night's contest. Some Sundays were unpleasant, even in winning situations, because of the breakdown in some areas of the team. There were always corrections and learning opportunities for players and coaches.

This millennium also inspired spiritual growth for me. In 2006, during another hectic football season, Beth pilgrimed to Medjugorje, a small town in Bosnia-Herzegovina, where apparitions of the Virgin Mary have been appearing to three visionaries daily since 1981. She went with a small group from our Catholic Church to pray for our family, marriage, and our vocations. Her first visit was in the mid-80s, and she vowed to return at some point. She felt like she was called to return and did so amid our crazy busy lives. One of her many prayer requests in her spiritual journey was that I someday would convert to Catholicism. At that time, I had been attending the Catholic Church with Beth since 1991, but I never felt the urge to go through the Rite of Christian Initiation for Adults program (RCIA) to convert. This program took about nine months to complete, so converting to Catholicism was not an easy feat.

I grew up in the Episcopal Church and felt like that was close enough. Early in life, I was raised in the Episcopal Church largely because my mom was Methodist and my dad was a cradle Catholic. After they were married in the Catholic church, they agreed to meet halfway and give the Episcopal Church a shot. I had always considered myself a Christian, but with my extensive history of going to Catholic mass, I had considered becoming Catholic but was not fully committed to go through the process. Beth never put pressure on me to convert, but she strongly indicated that we were raising our future children Catholic after we were married. I could sense this was a deal-breaker if I bucked this one.

Beth traveled to the former Yugoslavia, and roughly five days into it, I began having reoccurring dreams about becoming Catholic. Between the lack of communication capabilities and the time zones, my conversations with Beth were extremely sparse, and we didn't speak of my dreams until she returned home.

Upon her return, I told her about the dreams and felt like the Holy Spirit was guiding me to join the church. "Beth, my dreams this week keep telling me it's time to join the family in Catholicism. Angel voices and other messages were directing my dreams."

She immediately started to cry. "Mike, I prayed every day for your conversion to the Catholic Church."

Soon after, I began the RCIA program at our church, and Beth was my faithful sponsor. Every week, we would meet at the church in a small group setting and learn about the history of the Catholic Church and the meaning of all the sacraments. The experience was extremely fulfilling, and we could look back at our lives and truly appreciate God's impact on some of our decisions that resulted from our prayer life. About a year later, I joined the Catholic Church.

She also prayed about the personal struggle she was having during endless hours that demanded my attention during football season. As her prayers were answered, she aligned her intentions with God to basically give it up during the season. The time I spent away from our family would affect other families in a spiritual and productive way. As a high school football coach, there were endless opportunities to make a positive impact in the lives of the young men. On that trip, Beth came to terms with that through the power of prayer. From that point on, she felt at peace with my career switch.

CHAPTER 21

LET'S TALK FOOTBALL - "BROTHERS STYLE"

A S I BEGAN my coaching career at Christian Brothers High School, I felt like a teenager coaching for my first time like I did in 1982. Really, in my mind, there was very little difference except the size, speed, and overall talent of the players (okay, maybe a lot of difference). However, one thing I noticed that was not different was the passion that these guys had for the game. I was blessed to have coached eight years of middle school football at football powerhouse Germantown, and I got that familiar feeling right off the bat at CBHS. I will never forget when Coach Locastro wanted to introduce me to the team right after the last summer conditioning session.

When I showed up at CBHS, a terrible lightning storm had just passed, and he had gathered all the players into the basketball gym to run a drill called "sixteen the hard way." On a regular football field, it's the distance between the hash mark and the boundary (sideline). On the watch, you run that distance in continuation sixteen times. If one person can't make his time, your group runs it again, as many times as it takes. Talk about accountability. The pace is close to a full sprint to keep up.

As I walked up, they were moving in the gym to perform this last task before they went on a three-day weekend before football camp started on that following Monday. After witnessing the boys starting the sixteen-the-hard-way task, I could sense the work and determination these young men had immediately. After observing for twenty minutes, I noticed puddles of sweat. The gym at the time was at ninety degrees or above, and this was not coincidental. Locastro later told me that he cut the AC off long before the conditioning session had started, anticipating the possibility that thunderstorms might happen.

Well, it stormed. The temperature inside simulated the outdoors except there was zero breeze. I think the players would have preferred to run outside in the hot sun compared to inside in a 90-degree gym without any breeze.

While I followed the herd of football players into the gym, I heard one player say, "We are going to die in this gym today."

"Damn thunderstorms," mumbled another.

The looks on their faces indicated this was serious business, and they had been through this before.

There were eighty-five kids killing themselves in a hot gym, and I absolutely loved it. I was extremely happy and blessed to be a part of this team for the upcoming season. It reminded me immensely of my senior year, giving it up on the track running 200-meter timed sprints administered by Coach Smith.

"We win this thing in the fourth quarter!" Locastro demanded.

The look on the face of each player was the look of determination and of exhaustion. I'm not going to lie; there were a few looks of anger also. Locastro was not gaining friends at this point.

The gloves were off, and the players were brought in. After the conclusion of the sixteen-the-hard-way session and players were given the opportunity to hydrate a bit, I was called over to the team's breakdown.

Coach Locastro said, "Gentlemen, we have a new coach that will join us this fall in the classroom and on the field. I know you guys will like his passion and intensity. He won a state football championship in high school and has been coaching at the middle school level for eight years. Give it up for Coach Mike O'Neill!"

What timing, right? These guys were exhausted, drenched in sweat, and meeting one of the new coaches who would join them on Monday morning football camp to coach linebackers when two-a-day practices begin. I almost couldn't believe I made it to this point of starting my new career.

After the brief introduction, I kept it short and sweet.

"Coach Locastro was right. I won a state championship as a senior, and many believe it was the best high school team to ever come out of Memphis. What I had witnessed brought me back to my days as a senior, and the determination and commitment of grinding through a drill is what it takes to accomplish your goals. I'm extremely jacked about what I just saw. And what I saw was a true commitment and an incredible work ethic today. Nothing is guaranteed, but one thing's for sure: If you bring that passion every day, the opportunity to be successful will increase dramatically."

Now players were nodding in agreement. It was obvious these guys were itching to make a run at a state title. Christian Brothers' one and only title came in 1977 when, incidentally, I was at the goal line only three feet from where Ronnie Skinner reeled in a perfectly thrown end reverse pass to win the game with no time left on the clock.

"Chris," I said, as I made eye contact with Ronnie's oldest son, "I was the first one who jumped on your dad in the back of the Liberty Bowl end zone that started the greatest dogpile in Christian Brothers' history."

Chris, who was battling for the starting quarterback position, was smiling from ear to ear. The boys welcomed me immediately after that story, and we got off to a great start in 2001.

By 2003, I became the defensive coordinator, and my first game was against a very high-powered Melrose Wildcat squad that was scheduled to play in the Bridge Builder Kickoff on a hot August day. These guys were ranked preseason number one in the 5A Public School Division State rankings. That spring and summer, we were able to obtain seven films from the previous season and we visited college coaching clinics where Melrose coaches were holding sessions. After breaking film and absorbing this team's method of operation, we knew we had our work cut out for us.

That entire summer, we basically created a Melrose offensive playbook that included players, offers by colleges, and detailed scheme and formation information that our kids began getting schooled up on since spring practice in February of that year. At the time, Melrose had nine Division I football players, and they were loaded on offense. The local newspaper hyped them all summer with multiple articles and proclaimed them to be the top team in the state. All this hype got the attention of Coach Locastro, and we began our preparation that spring. We were happy to be playing the 5:00 p.m. game as well and hoped it would be as hot as ever. We knew we would win the conditioning battle. We had to; it was our only chance to stay in the game.

That entire summer was also dedicated to game one. The determination by our players and coaches was simply unmatched. That's all we talked about the entire summer.

Our guys were in fantastic condition heading into game week with Melrose. The local paper had them ranked #1 in the city and we were ranked #2. We didn't have nine Division I prospects, but we eventually sent two offensive linemen, one defensive end, and one tight end to the University of Memphis that next year. So, we weren't exactly hurting. However, we didn't have their team speed, and it was a nightmare trying to simulate it during the summer practices. What we didn't have in speed, we made up for it in conditioning. One goal was to get in the fourth quarter.

The Saturday morning of the Bridge Bowl Game, the local paper ran a front-page pictorial that included a pyramid of the top Melrose players with their South Carolina QB signee at the top with gold cleats on. I then quickly jumped in the car and scrambled to find about thirty copies and high-tailed it to CBHS and stuck them into lockers of the team. Each player had a copy taped to the top of his locker when he entered the locker room around midday. It was on! I knew our kids would be hyped out of their mind when they saw the spread the paper sent out that morning. Five of the six guys on that team pyramid were on offense, and the challenge was staring them right in the face.

The first drive of the game, our defense swarmed the mighty Melrose attack to set the tone. Our guys were flying to the ball every snap. On the sidelines between series, I was getting updates.

"Coach, we see it. We know what's coming every play, and they are frustrated that we know their plays," claimed a defensive captain.

As Melrose became frustrated, the penalties and personal fouls began to take a toll on their performance. The defense stifled the mighty Wildcat offense machine and only gave up one touchdown late in the third quarter.

Our only touchdown was scored by our defensive tackle, Ryan Williams, after he read middle screen deep inside the Melrose territory. Ryan picked it off at the one-yard line and hopped in the end zone to tie it up. Late in the game, we kicked a thirty-yard field goal to win, 10-7. Our fourth quarter stamina was the difference, and Melrose put together only one significant drive the entire game.

Our players could see the surprise from the Melrose offensive because we would call out their formation lingo based on information obtained from a coach's clinic. Our Defensive Line Coach Jim Dotson attended an Ole Miss football camp and took great notes on what the Melrose offensive coordinator presented. There was nothing done illegally or unethically. We took it to the next level in preparation. That day, we shocked the state!

Chris Walker, a defensive end prospect later in my career, was recruited heavily by almost everyone! The big-time programs liked his raw size and athletic ability to move and run. Chris, at six foot four, could run a 4.5 forty that gained a ton of attention from the SEC and other power five conferences.

That winter, before the February signing date, head coaches came for school visits. Big 10, Pac 12, and Big 12 recruiting coordinators would frequently visit the campus, trying to cash in on the Chris Walker lottery. Just before signing day, Chris gave a verbal agreement to Phillip Fulmer with the University of Tennessee after the coach paid him a home visit.

The very next week, the University of Alabama's top recruiter Kevin Steele reached out to Coach Locastro to announce that he and Head Coach Nick Saban were in route and wanted to come see Chris Walker on campus before the signing date on that Tuesday. Coach Steele announced they would be there in two hours and to have Chris ready to get out of class. They were about to board a plane for Memphis and Chris Walker was one of the first athletes who Coach Saban attempted to sway to Tuscaloosa as he took over the head position at Alabama. Coach Locastro informed Steele that Chris had already given a verbal to Tennessee before they took off; however, that wasn't a concern for the two Crimson Tide coaches.

Like clockwork, Coach Saban and Coach Steele arrived at the front office during fifth period. I was thrilled because that was my off period, and I was invited to join the meeting along with a couple of the freshman coaches who happened to have fifth off as well. The buzz around school had gotten out that Alabama Coach Nick Saban would be on campus, even though Coach Locastro attempted to keep it on the down low as much as possible.

Our staff was quickly briefed in the coach's office and basically provided simple ground rules for the meeting about to take place. "Okay, guys," Locastro said. "Let's keep our mouths shut and hear Alabama's sales pitch and, above all, no stupid questions."

The office intercom announced, "Coach Locastro, the Alabama staff has arrived. Can you meet them in the front office?"

"Here we go. I'll be right back."

Five minutes later, Kevin appeared with Nick Saban and Kevin Steele to the rather cramped coach's office on the north side of the campus. As the three men entered the office, the excitement was palpable. This was Coach Saban's first stop in Memphis after being introduced as the Crimson Tide's new head coach.

"Coach Locastro, we have about twenty-five minutes before our next stop," Coach Steele, the Tide's defensive coordinator, announced as the men made their way in. Everyone took a seat around the rectangular table.

After brief introductions took place and a bit of small talk, we went right to business. Coach Saban wanted to meet Chris within five minutes of arrival because of their tight schedule; however, what Coach Saban didn't know was that Chris wasn't exactly ready to meet with him. All morning, Walker indicated to Coach Locastro that he gave his word to Coach Fulmer and that was that. Chris said he knew there was a good chance he might get talked into playing for Alabama if he left his fifth period English class. Locastro went to retrieve Walker out of class but to no avail. All morning, he was going back and forth with this decision but decided he was staying put.

After Kevin came back to the coach's office, he spoke to the two coaches in a direct somber tone. "Coach Saban, Chris will not leave English class to meet with you. He reminded me that he gave his verbal to Tennessee yesterday and that's where he plans to go."

The room had the feeling of a mortuary, and the look on Coach Saban's face was not pleasant. If you're a sports fan, you have probably seen that look on his face during a post-game press conference after a ridiculously dumb question by a sports reporter.

"Does he know he's going to miss out on several national championships if he doesn't come to Alabama? Coach, I'm not leaving until Walker comes out to talk with me."

Dead silence filled the room. By that time, Locastro explained that he will try again, but he felt like Chris already made up his mind.

Upon Kevin's exit, Coach Saban was now pacing the room. After a bit, Kevin returned once again, Walker free.

"Coach Saban, I apologize, but Chris has made up his mind and will not leave class to meet with you."

"Get him out here, coach!" Saban demanded.

"Coach, I'm not going to force him out here if he refuses."

Coach Saban was back to pacing and shaking his head continuously in disgust. After he explained a few other reasons why Walker should come to Alabama, he and Coach Steele were off to the next school.

Man, was that intense! I will hand it to Coach Locastro in not making Walker come against his wishes and Chris keeping his word to Tennessee. However, in hindsight, Chris would be sporting three National Championship Rings with the Crimson Tide had he left his English class.

We had some good teams at Christian Brothers and in 2005, we played for the D-AA Large Private School State Championship vs. our rival Memphis University School on the campus of Middle Tennessee State University in Murfreesboro. Both schools tried to convince the Tennessee Secondary School Athletic Association (TSSAA) to move the game to the Liberty Bowl, but they would have nothing to do with it. The game would be played at Floyd Stadium. We were ranked #1 in the state with the #1 defense. MUS was ranked #2 with a prolific offense.

After a great week of practice, we went to compete for a state title, not achieved by our school in twenty-eight years. This time, a defensive battle it was not. Unfortunately, it was a track meet from the start. After going back and forth with several lead changes, we had a drive stall in the MUS red zone to seal the game. On third and six, a tipped ball on a pass route landed in the hands of a MUS defensive back at their own fifteen-yard line. Everything was clicking along that drive until a mystery holding call stalled, and we elected to throw a crossing route and it was picked deep in Owl territory. MUS had eighty-five yards to go with two minutes left in the game. This drive was a defensive coordinator's worst nightmare. The #1 defense in the state had the wheels completely fall off the wagon for the last two minutes. The drive included two personal foul penalties that extended two drives and one fourth and ten that turned into a fourth and five when a defensive end lined up in the neutral zone at the fifty-yard line. Of course, the next play, MUS completed a five-yard play action pass to a running back in the flats for another set of downs. MUS went on to score the game-winning drive with twenty-five seconds left on the clock. That defeat was the toughest game in my coaching history ever to digest. Those kids had a great season, and I love them all, but that was a very tough pill to swallow.

My last season at CBHS was in 2008. The summer prior to the 2009 season, Coach Locastro and I didn't see eye to eye on some issues, so I decided to shift gears and look for new opportunities. It was unfortunate my time at Christian Brothers High School would end like that. I did, however, appreciate all my experiences and the contacts I made over the years and wouldn't change that for anything.

CHAPTER 22

THE TRANSITION TO THE 'VILLE'

'M NOT GOING to sugarcoat it; 2009 was a rough year. That summer, leading up to the season, I made the choice of shifting gears from a coaching perspective. I informed the administration at CBHS that I was stepping out of coaching football for the 2009 season because of differences I had with the head coach. For me professionally, it was time for a change. I enjoyed teaching at CBHS and realized when I made the decision not to coach, I would eventually pursue other coaching/teaching opportunities elsewhere. I talked it over with Beth and informed her it was time to make that move; however, it couldn't have been worse timing. My son Michael, a rising sophomore and whom I had been waiting years to coach at the high school level, was the fly in the ointment.

At times, professional growth and personal wants don't always correlate, and I was learning that the hard way. Michael came off a solid freshman year and won the starting role as offensive center and provided solid minutes as a defensive end, so his future was bright. However, professionally, things happened in the off-season that forced me to think about my long-term goals. I knew the role of head coach would be a distinct possibility in my future but knew at CBHS Coach Locastro was my age and had done a sound job with no intention of leaving. Furthermore, I wanted to be in a place where I could help grow and move in the right direction and realized Kevin and I had different philosophies on that point. It was no one's fault, and there was no right or wrong. It was time to unhook my cart and move in another direction. Beth saw it coming for some time and seemed relieved I was branching out.

Now the hurdle was Michael. He was off to a great start academically and made a ton of new friends, but he was recovering from a torn labrum in his right shoulder that happened at the end of his freshman football season. Because of that, his baseball career was over, and he really worked hard in the off-season to endure an intense sophomore campaign in the ensuing months. One of the perks at Christian Brothers was the 100-percent free tuition for teacher's kids. At the time, they were the only private school in Memphis that offered that deal, so I guess it made up for the lack of a coach's stipend they offered to assistant coaches. My problem was extremely complex and confusing, but I just felt the time was now for a change.

The 2009 school year was unique because it was the first time in a very long while where I was once again football-free. I still taught six classes, but I didn't have my responsibilities directly after school. The administration and head baseball coach tried to talk me into coaching baseball, but I knew it would be my last year at CBHS. The entire year was kind of strange, but especially during the football season. I really missed being out there with Michael and the rest of the team during his sophomore campaign.

Even though the year was out of the ordinary, it provided an opportunity to participate and expand my dad duties. By this time, Brooke was at UT Knoxville, and Mary was a freshman at St. Agnes. That year, I was able to take her to and from school every day and then take the twenty-five-minute drive back to the Brothers to get Mike post-practice.

As I was able to increase my parental duties, I missed being on the sidelines. Obviously, the players had a ton of questions about my departure and asked repeatedly why I wasn't on the staff anymore, and they were hammering Mike for as much information as possible. The kids in my class were asking nonstop, and the rumor mill was out of control.

Many times, while about to begin a lesson, I would hear:

"Coach, will you be at Collierville next year? They need a coach."

"Coach, I heard you will be on the staff next year at Memphis."

"Coach, is it true you got fired?"

"No, no, and no," I responded without detail. Students were extremely inquisitive throughout the semester, especially the players. No telling what they heard on their end, but my stance was I kept my mouth shut while seeking other opportunities.

That entire time was weird, and that season could not come and go fast enough. During the downtime, I was able to get my resume updated and put some feelers out. The word had gotten out that I was in the market as I began to network with some other schools. I didn't let the administration in on it, but I think they started to catch on. However, teams were in the middle of their seasons and were not in the market for coaches. In education, the early spring months is when that movement happens. Teacher contracts usually happen in the spring and jockeying for additional coaches on staff will usually begin in January to April. Overall, the fall of 2009 was football-grind-free, and it was an excellent chance to reset and contribute on the home front.

As the fall of 2009 ended, I began to intensify my networking. I was open to private school, but I kept up with my teacher's license if an opportunity opened on the public school side. That fall, I was able to update and get my license renewal for another ten years so now the public school system was a distinct possibility. Most private schools don't require a license to teach, but the public schools will not grant you an interview without one. I spoke to many people on the coaching front, but again, hands were tied until teacher contracts came out.

Schools simply must equate how many new positions are open compared to current teachers enrolled to return or get fired. Also, student enrollment will dictate how many teaching positions are available.

So, with the turn of the new year, my search expanded and so did the rumor mill about my future. One place I considered was my hometown high school: Collierville. Recently, Coach Paul Cox had retired, and there was a lot of interest in that job from a public perspective. I threw my name in the hat, knowing it was a long shot. Insiders were leaning toward an internal hire; however, I thought it would be good experience to push my resume and sent a heartfelt email to Dr. Tim Setterlund. Tim was the vice principal at Germantown back when Coach Netherland and Principal Chism lined me up with an interview to determine how much school I would need to get licensed as a business teacher. Hence, I didn't obtain an interview, but I did receive a nice email from Dr. Setterlund stating he remembered our meeting and wished us continued success in the future. He did inform me they were leaning toward an internal hire, and he kept his word. Coach Shawn Abel, a longtime assistant coach to Coach Cox, was announced as the new Collierville Dragon head football coach. No surprise there! Shawn had done his time and was a terrific ball coach.

While my attention was focused elsewhere that winter, I had to keep in mind on where my son would ultimately wind up. In a perfect world, I would love it if he transferred with me to wherever I landed. However, I told him he was certainly free to stay at CBHS and I didn't want to interfere or wreck his high school experience. I made that completely clear to him. Even with my departure, I felt like the staff would give him a fair shake to play his junior and senior years. At the same time, Beth and I were not going to let him go to a school that wouldn't challenge him academically.

I wanted to make sure Michael understood my position and career moves were separate from how I felt as a father. My priority was him, and if that meant he stayed and eventually graduated CBHS in 2012, I wanted him to have ownership in this decision. So, Plan A, he would stay and graduate from Christian Brothers unless things lined up in the next couple months. By this time, it was March, and I didn't have a clear picture of where I would go. The next few weeks I went on some interviews; however, moving forward, I needed to intensify and expand my search. The pressure was on.

It was early April on a Saturday afternoon when the doorbell rang at my house in Collierville. When I opened the door, I saw a man who appeared to be a football coach sporting a Collierville football coaches shirt.

"Hey, I'm Shawn Abel. I'm looking for Mike O'Neill. Am I at the right house?"

"Yes, you found it," I said as I looked at Beth.

"Great, Mike. I'm the head football coach at Collierville High School."

Now it started to click. This was Collierville's new hire. I now recognized him from the multiple media stories that the local TV stations and newspaper ran on him. I had never met him in person, so I wasn't sure when I first saw him. I quickly invited him in. Beth was kind of thrown off until he explained his new position as Collierville head coach. Within a couple minutes, we were in the kitchen talking high school football and connecting the dots. After a bit of small talk, he jumped right to it. "Mike, we have a mutual acquaintance, an ex-coach to both of us, and he informed me that you were now in the market beyond Christian Brothers."

I hadn't the faintest idea about who he was talking about.

"Rocky Graves," he said. "Rocky Graves coached you at Germantown and coached me at Rhodes College back in the mid-80s."

Wow. At that time, I was wracking my brain to figure out how and when Coach Graves learned about my availability to coach. Coach Graves was the offensive coordinator in the state champion run during my senior year. The following year, he and Coach Leland Smith went to Rhodes College to coach at the collegiate level.

"I'm in the market for a defensive coordinator and strength coach for the 2010 football season. Coach Graves called me yesterday about your availability and felt confident that you had not committed to any school at this point."

As he was giving his sales pitch, I could see the excitement and interest on Beth's face. Looking back, I shared the same excitement about what I was hearing coming out of Coach Abel's mouth. I thought this would be a perfect fit for Michael. Collierville has an excellent reputation as a college preparatory high school that would challenge Mike in the classroom. Dr. Setterlund was clearly an academic-driven principal first and foremost. Mike was still very connected to friends in Collierville. As a little guy, he went to grade school at Tara Oaks, and I knew he had several buddies whom he kept in contact with on the football team.

"Hey, let's get in the car and go to the weight room," Shawn insisted.

This unscheduled interview was getting better and better. As we climbed into the car and took off, it took all of three minutes to arrive at the football complex just about one mile from my driveway.

"No commute, Mike."

It would probably be another twenty-six minutes until I arrived at Christian Brothers. Now Coach Abel really had my attention, and he was laying it on thick. As we walked through the doors of the Paul Cox Center, Shawn continued the sales pitch. "I need a strength coach that has passion and vision to update the weight room and the program." The weight room appeared to be stuck in the early nineties. As we continued the tour, he informed me that he liked my reputation as a defensive coordinator.

"You are given the freedom to install your system as you see fit based on the current personnel offered by the current Collierville talent pool."

At that moment, I was still thinking about a new strength and conditioning program to install while he was talking.

He then stated, "I'm not a micromanager and need a DC that will run with it."

He explained he was the current offensive coordinator along with being the head coach. "I need someone to be able to walk in and teach our kids a new defensive philosophy and a strength coach that will motivate our guys to another level."

By this time, I'm grinning ear to ear. This guy who walked in my life about thirty minutes ago was hitting all the buttons, and I was getting fired up. He then informed me about two additional stipends would come beyond teaching! Wow, I was thinking this was too good to be true. I didn't even know stipends existed. At CBHS in the 2000s, they weren't given to full-time teachers who coached.

After the athletic facility tour, we made our way back to the house as Shawn continued his presentation. "Collierville has transformed into a baseball school for several reasons, and it's imperative we rebuild the youth football program that collapsed a few years ago. It won't be easy."

He informed me of several challenges the football program would face in the next year but was excited to once again get it going in the right direction. Upon returning home, he wanted to come back inside to gauge my interest, and I informed him he had my complete attention. I then called Mike down to meet Coach Abel.

"Mike, meet Coach Abel. Coach here is the head coach at Collierville High School."

"Oh, he'll do nicely," Shawn said as he looked over Mike's frame and demeanor. "We need major help up front in this new offense. You ever played guard?"

"Yes, sir," Mike quickly replied.

Coach Abel and Mike hit it off. We discussed details, and then we shook hands. I thanked him for dropping by and for the tour.

After Coach Abel departed, Beth, Michael, and I looked at one another in disbelief about what had just transpired. Beth informed Mike and I that last week she'd had a recent dream about us both going to Collierville next year.

"The Holy Spirit must be hard at work," she said as she crossed herself.

We invited Michael in on the conversation, and he spoke up immediately and made it crystal clear. "Dad, I'm going where you are going. I want to be coached by you!"

My heart was filled with joy when he spoke, and tears began to flow. That night, I called Coach Abel and said Mike and I are in if you can get it done on your side. He then told me he'd already been working on it since he left my house. He said he'd picked up on the buying signals earlier that day that I was interested in pursuing an opportunity at Collierville.

Over the next couple weeks, Coach Abel began seeking out opportunities in the classroom with the hope I could become the defensive coordinator and head strength coach for his program in his first season as head coach.

In the ensuing week, Coach Abel built his case to Dr. Setterlund about expanding the business curriculum due to the fact that many college-bound kids wanted to major in business. Also, Doc told Shawn he would help him with his first hire to get things going in the right direction. Coach kept me in close contact and talked me up with the administration.

By the end of April, I was granted an interview for a position in the CTE Department teaching Intro to Business Accounting and Marketing for the fall of 2010. I was thrilled and the timing was near perfect. My time at CBHS was ending because I had put off the administration about coaching other sports long enough.

My interview was scheduled for a Friday morning, so I took a personal day from Christian Brothers. I needed this position for stability and growth in my career, but more importantly, it would provide a successful experience for Michael in the classroom and on the football field. This interview was critical.

My first meeting was with the chairperson of the CTE Department. Next, I then went into Dr. Setterlund's office. Shawn was right when he stated the interview process at Collierville High School was serious business. I wasn't surprised; I knew it would be thorough, and

I was prepared. As the second interview began, Dr. Setterlund made note of my email from a few months ago and our first meeting some twenty years ago at Germantown High School. Upon recalling our conversation, he noticed on my resume that I pursued business for ten years after our meeting. He then stated, "I must have done a great job selling you on being a teacher, right?"

After we broke the ice, he jumped right into his question. "If I were to pull a student out of one of your business classes at CBHS and ask him what kind of impact you have made in their life, how might they respond?"

Dr. Setterlund was not pulling punches. I liked that. "Dr. Setterlund," I responded, "my business students will tell you that Coach O'Neill has provided a base of understanding by successfully teaching the business curriculum with zeal and the combination of real-world business experience to enhance every lesson."

The interview was a success.

Early that next week, I had a contract offer in the mail. Michael was extremely excited about going to Collierville and was eager to work with the new staff, including his dad. Coach Abel liked Michael's size and desperately needed a physical offensive pulling guard to help his new offensive scheme. My plan was to have him on defense also because of his aggressive nature.

The 2009-2010 school year was difficult on the entire family. However, it subsequently ended on a great note moving into the summer before Michael's junior year. I was able to get transfer eligibility with the Tennessee Secondary School Athletic Association (TSSAA) for Mike. The rule is good for a teacher who transfers schools and can bring their child over to the next campus without any penalty. This applies to only one transfer to prevent coaches from school hopping with their athlete over and over. Perfect! Mike was eligible, and it was time to go back to work. He could not join the team until the academic school year was over. However, I joined the team directly after I signed my new contract to teach at Collierville. Soon after I started,

I was able to evaluate the weight program, equipment, and players. I would officially begin my strength/conditioning program June 1.

Mike and I were ready to take it to the next level. Over the next few weeks, I acclimated to Dragon football and began to push toward the 2010 football season as their defensive coordinator and head strength coach!

CHAPTER 23

DRAGON TIME

T HE EXHILARATION I experienced with my new position at Collierville High School was off the charts. Now I could teach and coach right in my backyard at one of the state's largest public high schools. I wanted to help build the football program in every way possible. Until the moment I got on board, Collierville football had never won a state championship in football. The closest was the 1973 season when the Dragons played in a AA State Game but lost. In the late '90s, the Dragons made a decent run to lose in the semifinals. The legendary Coach Paul Cox had an impressive overall record with 280 wins, but in recent years, the program began to take a few steps back. One of the biggest challenges was the lack of participation at the youth football level. Over time, due to the liability of concussions and the mismanagement of resources, the city of Collierville decided they were getting out of the tackle football business.

As the supply and demand began to erode youth football, a major transition to youth baseball for top youth athletes went to a whole other level. Now in the fall, the city offered Youth Wooden Bat Baseball leagues and only flag football for the Gridiron community.

In 2010, the Collierville football program had its challenges, but it also had some of the last set of CYAA players who were currently seniors and played in the youth league when it was at its peak as little guys. The 2010 team had some solid talent that was fundamentally sound and had an adequate amount of multi-sport athletes. On paper, we had a good mix of athletic kids and a decent amount of size; however, I felt this group needed a bit more focus and drive in order to make a run in the playoffs.

My first task as the strength coach that spring was to redesign the strength/conditioning program currently being used. The current program was a bit outdated—only three days a week, requiring zero lifting to maintain what was accumulated in the off-season. Also, the weight equipment and layout were average and required transformation but would need to wait until the next off-season. There were so many things to consider but knowing that fall football camp was just two short months away, the focus on the short term was vital.

During my first week at Collierville, I wasted no time and implemented a program I was very familiar with. Over the past ten years at CBHS, I was actively involved in the program run by the head strength coach, Mark Hamer, who played for Coach Leland Smith while at Rhodes College in the early '90s and was a direct descendant of Coach Smith in terms of strength & conditioning philosophy. Mark and I had traveled to several strength clinics over the years, and he was a goldmine of information and knowledge.

Over the years, I was trying to sponge up all information because I knew, at some point, I would be put in a position to implement a dynamic strength/conditioning program. That time was now. That summer we went to a four-day split program and would test every player from the start. That included weight, vertical jump, forty, and the main Olympic lifts (including cleans, squats, and bench). In week two, I had posters of percentages needed so those players could quickly glance and load up the exact amount of weight based on their percentage of their last current max.

We also amped up the speed training with days dedicated to fast twitch muscle movement and other days focused on pure conditioning and cardio work based on the strength exercises worked that day. At first, players weren't too sure about the change, but as the midsummer mandatory dead period kicked in, guys were buying into the new program.

The other challenges I quickly determined were the two sport athletes (baseball/football) we currently had and how the number of dual-sport players must improve to get this program where it needed to be. Basically, I didn't see many baseball kids until summer ball was finished. Even then, many more opted out of playing football in the fall and that trend would only accelerate as time moved forward. Some of these players were involved in travel teams that lasted right until the first game. That being the case, these players were not allowed to join the football team that fall. It was obvious the two sports were working against one another, especially leading up to football season.

Coach Abel clearly understood the disconnect between the programs and the major problems it presented. Abel also understood the disconnect between the middle school programs and the transition to high school. Two things were obvious: (1) some top-tier athletes were simply going to other schools for athletic reasons, and (2) some athletes were simply losing interest or motivation to play football beyond eighth or ninth grade. We had a ton of these students walking the halls at Collierville. We must give or a provide a reason to stay at Collierville or simply play football at the varsity level. We had to make football "the thing to do once again in Collierville." We needed to make football more marketable and inspire potential student athletes to want to join and be a part of the team. In the meantime, we needed to push the rest of the student body to get our home stadium rocking again on Friday nights to help aid in creating the excitement for football.

It was beyond critical to update the facilities as the opportunity of a new school was on the horizon. In 2010, we needed to freshen up what we currently had to keep and attract athletes from the surrounding area. Currently, the football stadium and weight room were about three miles off campus from the high school behind Collierville Elementary School.

Herman Osteen Field was built in the '60s and the wooden bleachers and scoreboard had to be continuously fixed. Furthermore, our 6A high school had a stadium with only a capacity of 2,300 people. The football locker room (connected to the elementary school gym) was about a 400-yard walk to the stadium and another seventy-five yards to the practice fields. The locker room was severely under capacity and downright dangerous at times, especially as numbers approached ninety players. On a heavy rain day, multiple leaks were throughout the locker areas so walking around in cleats was quite hazardous. Also, any mold testing device would probably have the place condemned and shut it down.

Over time, the booster club and local businesses created the Paul Cox Athlete Training Center, which took some pressure off the locker room and was a step in the right direction. This change happened back in the early 2000s, but now the weight facility needed updating with better equipment. This would happen in the next off-season with a goal to work out eighty kids at a time in a safe and functional manner. In 2010, the weight complex and the natural grass field were probably the highlight of the grounds. Synthetic turf would have been ideal, but every season Coach Mike Bradley had the football field looking like a fairway at Augusta or Pebble Beach. He maintained it, and the rest of the coaches helped him paint it and it looked immaculate for Friday night games. With all the setbacks and missed opportunities to change the facilities in the past, the explosion in growth in the town of Collierville was approaching 50,000 by 2010.

As my career at Collierville High School continued, I was able to adjust conditions and attitudes toward football during my tenure. Change can be painful but also a growth opportunity if you keep the big picture in mind. As the summer before the 2010 season began, I had time to install my multiple 4-2-5 defense with different looks, and my guys were excited about the new scheme and the detailed game plans they were provided in the process. As time went on, their football intellect began to improve.

As we approached the season, I could tell most of the guys were buying in and craved the discipline they were getting as the season started. The 2010 team made it to the second round of the playoffs and lost to Germantown in a packed Herman Osteen Field and won eight games that season. Notably, that was the first playoff run in twelve years and had the best raw talent and overall interior lineman size in my tenure at CHS. The following season started a very long drought of small interior linemen on the offensive/defensive sides of the football. On the upside, the players we currently had were getting stronger with the updated strength program; however, the natural girth of players were getting smaller over time.

As a coach, you cannot help but measure team size. In the film room, looks can be deceiving, especially when camera angles are from far away. Unless you scout a team in person, you are never quite sure about team size of your opponent overall. Size certainly isn't everything, but occasionally it would be nice to be the bigger guy in the room.

After class, I would take off for five minutes to comb the building until the next bell. Walking through the packed hallways at our undersized building was always a challenge, but I could see a ton of students in the process. My goal was to seek out potential students who appeared to be athletic but were not currently with the football program. I would get directly to the point. "Have you ever played football, or are you interested in joining the football program?" This was generally my approach, and the answers varied.

"I work."

"Tried it in freshman year and didn't like it."

"I play baseball only."

"I play basketball only."

"Mom won't let me."

"Maybe. I'll give it some thought."

It was simply a numbers game. On occasion, I had recruited basketball kids for receivers or running backs, wrestlers for all positions, and usually I was successful in convincing soccer players to handle our kicking game. Over time, we had outstanding placekickers and punters who had resulted from those hallway recruiting adventures.

I eventually allowed the baseball team to use the football weight facility to gain trust and maintain the strength of the dual football/baseball player. It was calculated, I know, but when we first started to let baseball players come in the football weight room, I was floored by witnessing the overall size of the kids walking through the door. Yes, the baseball kids incidentally were taller and broader than football players. As they showed up for their baseball workout, I introduced myself along with some direct questions as they filed in.

"Ever played football?

"Any interest in football?

"Would you like to give football a shot?"

Most of the answers I received were to the point.

"No, sir, never played."

"Not interested."

"I play one sport."

"Parents won't let me. Too dangerous."

"Don't want to lose my scholarship by getting hurt."

This problem was major and far worse than I expected. Overcoming it and sharing our best athletes seemed like it would be more challenging in the future. Over time, this mentality needed to shift if the football program was to compete on a championship level.

The 2011 season was a rough one on multiple levels. Losing kids to graduation the previous spring turned out to be the largest obstacle to overcome for several reasons: speed, offensive linemen, and overall leadership were in short supply heading into the season.

Coach Abel was in his second year as a head coach after coming off a fantastic start to his tenure in taking his first squad to the second round of the 2010 playoffs. However, the 2011 season started to take a toll from the start. The off-season was solid, but over the summer, some of the baseball kids who played last season simply didn't want to play football any longer. After Hunter Bradley, an All-State tight end, was lost to an ACL injury one day before the start of the season, adjustments to the offense had to be made overnight, and the pressure was mounting quickly.

I just lost my top defensive player also. Hunter was a great defensive end but was a difference maker on offense. Basically, a tight end with wide out speed.

As the season began, we came out of the gate respectfully, winning the first three games. After that, we started a downward spiral and won only one out of the last seven games. Some were blowouts and others were hard fought. The first red flag of the season was beating a very average Hillcrest team 20-12 in a dogfight week one. After two more very narrow victories, future wins were extremely hard to come by. We lost to an eventual 2-8 Kirby team in the last minute to solidify a playoff berth. In my nine-year stint at Collierville, it was the worst loss by far.

The next week, we attempted to regroup against a very good Wooddale team at Halle Stadium, and the implosion began before the game even started. During pregame, before getting on the bus to take off to Halle, one of the players violated a team rule put in place before the season started: Unless medically necessary, spatting above the cleats was not permitted unless granted by the team trainer; otherwise, it was a major waste of time and resources. (Spatting is when the cleat and socks are taped on the outside.) However, one senior player went to the parking lot twenty minutes before we were to take the buses over to Halle Stadium and was getting both ankles spat by a rival player on the tailgate of a pickup truck just outside of the locker room.

Coach Abel was walking up from the stadium back to the locker room to ensure everything was ready for the thirty-minute drive. Just before he entered the locker room, he caught the two out of the corner of his eye and walked over to the truck.

"Get your ass in the locker room now! Who are you? You don't belong here."

At that point, Shawn burst into the coach's office with conviction. "Coaches, get all of the players in the locker room now before we take off to Halle!"

That's when Abel completely lost it. By that point, I could hardly blame him. At that moment in the season, it was week nine, and a large portion of the team had checked out, even though if we could pull off an upset win that night, we could get to the playoffs. However, over the past few weeks, some of the players were pushing Coach Abel's buttons, and with the stress of the season, everything hit a boiling point right before we were set to board the bus to play.

The infamous ass-chewing began in the parking lot with instruction for every player to be in the meeting room within two minutes. As mentioned before, this meeting room was quite small and cramming eighty guys into it was extremely tight.

While the kids were frantically gathering into the meeting room, Abel called for a coach's meeting in the office to update us on what had happened just as two Shelby County school buses arrived to load up the team.

"Time to reset attitudes and priorities moving forward," Abel said.

At that point, Abel and the entire staff felt like the team was slipping away. Practices were up and down, attitudes were sour, and the level of frustration was high. The week before, some JV players were unscrewing their cleats from the bottom of their shoes and throwing them at cars on Highway 385 coming back from a Monday JV game.

As the players piled into the meeting room, you could feel a general buzz of what was happening before the players arrived. The coaches weren't required to join the meeting, but I stood outside nervously pacing from side to side and within earshot. When all the players were gathered in the room, you could hear a pin drop and the tension was high. Shawn was the only coach in the room. Since the room was small, every kid would hear everything about to be communicated.

"I will have it done my way or your ass will be gone. *You* don't call the shots around here. That's what has been our problem all damn year! It's not age, it's not injury, it's not the officials—it's individuality! Go play golf!"

He simply painted a clear picture of what happened in the parking five minutes prior, and this was kind of a microcosm of what had been happening all season long. As the meeting went on, his voice became louder and his language more colorful.

"You think you're a man, stand up and be one. Don't try that shit behind my back," he yelled at the top of his voice. "I'm sorry to yell, but apparently you don't understand when I talk to you like a human! Figure this shit out."

That night the dominos began to fall. After the players received their marching order, they quickly boarded the bus and began a thirty-minute ride to Memphis to play the Wooddale Cardinals. The rain and cold weather that afternoon made for a soggy field. As the game began, our players seemed motivated for an upset and fought hard for four quarters but lost in an epic back-and-forth battle.

The season was over except for one more out-of-conference game the next week against a stellar Ridgeway team for senior night. On the bus ride home, emotions and tempers began to flare. Players on the defensive team buses were calling out one another; the offensive bus had a fight breakout as we hit the parking lot to the football complex. After we arrived, I was doing my rounds to keep the peace in the main locker room, as the arguing and blame game continued, when I heard loud voices.

"I need help!" yelled Coach Davis from the shower area as a group of players were going toe to toe. Things were getting heated once again. After we cooled that skirmish, more yelling came from the meeting room as two players were the midst of a donnybrook and now fists were flying. As the entire football staff separated all parties, a sense of order was finally established.

This was turning into the longest day on record. Coach Abel had to fill out incident reports, and one of the senior players was going to be suspended for hitting another player. The player who was reprimanded was forced to turn in his equipment that night and remove all his personal belongings immediately. That Friday was a complete shit show, and I finally crawled into bed around three a.m.

Over the weekend, Shawn worked nonstop. By Sunday at the coaches meeting, very little game planning, if any, was accomplished, and everything revolved around this incident. A handful of kids received a one-day suspension for their involvement, and one player was suspended from Friday night's game for hitting the other younger classman on the face. He also received a three-day out-of-school suspension.

On Monday morning everything came to a head. Just before first period started, I was informed by Michael that Coach Abel's message was now on YouTube. "What?" At that time, I didn't have a YouTube account but knew most high school kids were all over it.

"Wait, back up."

Then, he played the recording on his phone. It was crystal clear what had transpired and communicated in the team meeting. Well, the unofficial policy of keeping team business in the walls of the locker room was compromised. This thing was in the process of going viral. I listened for about ten seconds and then shot through the halls down to Abel's classroom. Just as I arrived, I found out he had stepped out. I told the kids in his first period to tell him to come to my room immediately. As I made my way back to the classroom, no less than six random students asked me if I heard what was posted on YouTube. I said nothing and kept walking. Just as I returned to my classroom, Shawn was at my door.

"I heard you wanted to see me. What's up?"

"Have you heard?"

"Heard what?"

His eyes were as big as saucers. Still holding Michael's phone, I told him to step outside, and I put the phone up and pressed play. The look on his face was complete and utter despair as he listened to the crystal-clear recording for about a minute. He then handed me the phone and began a crisp walk in the direction of the main office. I knew what Abel's next move would be: go tell the administration directly before they found out from another source.

Back in my classroom, I was fortunate to have Michael and a couple other football players in my accounting class. Today's lesson was put on hold, and I brought some of the players back to my desk to get to the bottom of what had happened. I was informed one of the players recorded the meeting. While the kid who was suspended for Friday night's senior night posted Coach Abel's speech on YouTube, I found out much later, multiple players had been recording team meetings for the past few weeks. That should tell you the mentality and the lack of team continuity we had that season. After the Kirby game, the wheels had begun to fall off the wagon; and in my opinion, it was what started the downward spiral for the 2011 Collierville football season.

That morning, the wagon fell off the cliff. About halfway through first period was when I received a message from an office runner to go straight to Dr. Setterlund's office. Mrs. Bradley would watch my class until I returned from the meeting. As I entered Doc's office, I noticed Coach Abel wasn't anywhere to be found. Dr. Setterlund asked me to take a seat and he came over and shut the door. I was now certain this had to do with the YouTube posting. After a brief pause, Dr. Setterlund informed me Coach Abel was on his way down to Shelby County Schools' Central Office to meet with the superintendent. *Damn, that can't be a good thing,* I thought. He then asked me if I heard the You-Tube of Coach Abel's pregame talk.

"Yes, sir. My son, Michael, told me about it, and I immediately went to Coach Abel's room to inform him about what had transpired. I then went back to class to get ready for first period."

"Well, Coach Abel has resigned from his position as head coach, and he strongly recommends that you become the interim to get us through the rest of the football season as well as the banquet the first week in December."

I was in complete shock and attempted to digest what just happened.

"I cannot provide any details on Shawn's behalf, but he will no longer be coaching football for the remainder of the season."

He asked me again if I were interested in fulfilling the task. At that time, my mind was going 100 mph.

"Yes, sir, I am willing to help the program in any way possible."

"Fine, take two periods off and get your plan ready for how you will approach the game on Friday."

As he began to stand from behind his desk, he then said, "We will have a team meeting in the cafeteria at the beginning of eighth period, and I will inform the team about the change. Thank you, Coach O'Neill. Oh, and one last thing: Let's leave the press out of this. We will administer a statement from Central Office, and that's all they need."

"Yes, sir. I will get our guys refocused on Ridgeway and reinforce your demands about not speaking to the press."

Immediately, I went back to my classroom, informed Mrs. Bradley that I was to take second and third period off, and went directly to the library. One thing was for sure: I didn't have a second to waste, and I knew I needed to formulate a game plan with little distraction. I understood come eighth period, any further attempted planning would be fruitless because of the anticipated reaction the entire program was about to receive. Not only did we lose our head coach, but we also lost our offensive coordinator. By then, I went directly to the coach's office to begin my breakdown on Ridgeway's defense. Fortunately, over the weekend, I did my usual game prep on Ridgeway offense, and they were beyond loaded, and we could be in serious trouble with our lack of speed and size. It wasn't even close. I'd hope on the defensive side they had some weaknesses, but they were as big as any high school team I've seen going back to Melrose in the early 2000s. After two hours of watching film, their defense was loaded with athletic talent but simple with scheme.

When I returned by fifth period, I now found out Coach Abel was not only relieved of his football duty but now suspended from the classroom until further notice. Shawn taught advanced math and was excellent in the classroom. My head was spinning and in complete disbelief. I still couldn't believe someone would record a team meeting in the sanctity of a high school football locker room. In the age of cell phones, more and more things like this were starting to happen.

That week was almost a complete blur also. I was crawling into bed around 1:30 a.m. every night, trying to coordinate practice, form the game plan, and continue to motivate players to have a great week of practice and give it up. Overall, my goal was to finish this season with high energy on a positive note, win or lose.

We didn't waste any time preparing for the game. While the offensive staff was standing up at the white board, multiple conversations and strategies were going on. We spent the first hour of practice installing sets and working on signals to distribute to the offense to create our tempo. We increased our short passing combo routes, jet sweeps, and speed options to get on to parameter more and installed a couple of trick plays. We went in with an attitude that we had nothing to lose, and our kids had an excellent week. On the defensive side, we simply tried to put eight in the box to slow their Pro I offense with great pad level and gang tackling. And, yes, try to create turnovers every down. We needed several turnovers to create short fields.

Thursday's walk-through arrived in record time. This was my first taste of being at the helm, and the week was refreshing. Even with the news vans and the occasional helicopter circling the practice field, the staff kept the players so occupied during the week they barely noticed the zoo around them. By midweek, the YouTube clip had made it to the Howard Stern Show. I will say that week our kids and staff remained focused and driven to put up a great fight with our giant opponent.

Friday night started with senior night at pregame. Along with being the interim head coach and defensive coordinator, I now was a dad in line waiting for my senior to be introduced while Beth and I got a picture taken with Michael pregame. During the week, I felt sad about Michael's imminent departure from the Dragon program but had to suppress it with 100 different distractions leading up to kickoff. I did all I could to keep it together in the moments leading up to play against the most talented team of the season, and the realization of coaching my son one last time.

The pregame festivities were perfect on an unusually warm late October night. The game, on the other hand, was not. Not even close. Offensively, we were committed to a fast tempo to see if Ridgeway could adjust properly to our multiple formations. Early in the game, we had some success and scored early, but for much of the contest, they stifled us. At first, they didn't adjust to most of the different formations and had overall success with their base formation throughout the game. But with their size, speed, and overall athletic ability, we were no match for them. The high tempo offense turned to three and out most series, and their possessions were extremely successful. Their Pro I offense hammered us on counter trey and toss sweeps and only threw five passes.

The 2011 Ridgeway game resulted in a blowout win for the visiting team. It was an extremely long night after a tough and long week, compounded by a dismal year for CHS Football. That Sunday, we cleaned out our lockers and began the off-season.

CHAPTER 24

AN OFF-SEASON LIKE NO OTHER

MY FIRST TWO years at Collierville were extremely fast paced. I taught six classes with four preps. I was a traveling teacher, which meant I traveled from room to room to conduct class. I felt like an Olympic Bobsledder going to class, pushing my gear. And trust me, these rooms were spread out all over the school. Usually, first year teachers are forced to do this because of the lack of classrooms in this now converted high school originally built to accommodate a middle school population and parking.

Year one was also intense because of my new roles as strength and conditioning coach and defensive coordinator. The good news in the strength program is that kids were buying in. Our workouts were intense with very little downtime, and above all, we held our guys accountable. Each player had a file on him stating his current overall strength, weight, and speed, and he would test every two months to document gains. Test days were always exciting when players could see the fruit of their labor. I eventually required the players body fat percentage to be measured and interviewed each player about their personal nutrition and eating habits. Collierville football began to fuel itself properly. Players began to understand the importance of breakfast and eating right while they understood the importance of hydration.

As we were off to a good start in my first year, year two we took a couple steps back. There seemed to be a disconnect in the football program. Senior leadership was down, and the lack of motivation was apparent. The combination of which would ultimately take its toll on the second-year head coach.

In the classroom, I was beginning to get a bit of normalcy now that I had my own room, and I was down to three preps. I still had six classes, but eighth period was athletic study hall where players (mainly upperclassmen) could catch their workouts. Furthermore, that was positive because I had a bit of time to turn into a football coach to start my second job of the day. It's extremely hard to walk out of a classroom onto a football field within thirty minutes. The eighth period was designed for football players to get their vehicles after seventh period and head to the football complex roughly seven minutes away. Once they arrived, players would quickly change to begin lifting weights or pad up for practice. Then they took the 400-yard walk to the weight room or practice field.

Without a doubt, my first two years at Collierville offered possibilities for change and long hours. My commute was cut way down, so Beth and I were able to see each other more frequently and have the entire family join in meals most evenings.

After the last game in the fall of 2011, the opportunity to become head coach at Collierville High School was knocking at my door. The banquet was scheduled for December 4, and my job as interim coach would continue through the banquet. However, we had three mandatory dead weeks between players and coaches, established by the TSSAA, which is designed to provide everyone a breather until teams jump right into their off-season weight programs. This downtime allowed me to focus on the banquet.

That Monday, as the kids cleaned out their lockers, each player was provided a checklist of items to be accomplished, which included a list of awards in which they would nominate players who best fit those categories. I started making phone calls to secure a guest speaker with the hope of sending a positive message to our young men off the heels of a very disappointing year. This was a three-hour event, and it was my first experience prepping awards, programs, and organizing speeches. The booster club helped with decorations and food. There was an entire committee who worked and organized this throughout the year. Basically, the banquet was our version of the Academy Awards to celebrate the past season. That year, Beth helped me organize the senior video, which was a major undertaking itself. I've learned over the years the banquet is probably more for the moms and dads than anyone else. And yes, in 2011, I was a dad also.

Leading up to the banquet, the initial search process for head coach had started. The coaching pool was quite vast, and a list of candidates was building quickly. Outside candidates saw Collierville as an outstanding opportunity due to the growth and raw size of the student population. We were a 6A program with 2,700 students and projected to be 3,000 in a few short years.

Coming off the 2011 season, there was certainly room for improvement. I was granted an interview right after the season was over because I threw my name in the hat on the first day available. Internally, we have very few people who wanted to take the reins except a freshman coach or two. Quite frankly, I was shocked with the small amount of interest within the halls of our school. No other varsity coaches had an interest in taking over.

Over the next couple weeks, I was either informed of or personally saw several candidates at the main office to interview for the head football position. Often, between classes, I would get reports from various players and students that a potential candidate was on campus.

"Coach, I think I just saw someone come in to interview for the head job. When is it your turn?" a player would alert me.

"No worries, my time will come. It's a process, and this job is highly sought after."

Later, I learned there were dozens of on-campus interviews taking place and some candidates were not granted the opportunity to interview at all.

The entire time through the process, I felt like I was fully prepared for my interview with a clear vision for the direction of Collierville football.

As I sat next to the athletic director, across from Dr. Sutterlund in the principal's office, I told myself, *Make my case and the rest is in God's hands.* My nerves were in check, and I believed my plan to restart and build the football program into a state contender was legitimate and attainable in due time.

My message was plain and simple. I would do everything in my power to move this football program to the next level and work my tail off day in and day out. I would follow the rules and be extremely fair to coaches, players, and everyone else who supported the program, including the football alumni. My goal was to rebuild the youth program with or without the city's help and provide the players a reason to stay at CHS by not going to surrounding schools to fulfill their football needs. Yes, along with private schools, other public schools sometimes recruited also; but more importantly I realized within the halls of Collierville, the football team must work with the other sports programs to share athletes from the basketball, baseball, and lacrosse teams. My plan was to reciprocate and encourage football kids to wrestle, run track, or whatever sport they were interested in. During my first two years at Collierville, we started a growing trend of football players participating in lacrosse and more basketball kids played football.

For this football program to reach another level, it was beyond imperative that baseball players become part of our team. In the interview process, I made it clear to the administration that my goal was to have a great relationship with the baseball program and build trust with the players and coaches. Over the past few summers, the trend of football/baseball kids were declining, and I was determined to change this. Football was clearly paying the price. Part of my plan was to recruit from within and target students who might like to play football, even if their experience was minimal. The number of kids playing football were solid; however, we needed additional multisport athletes.

"It's crucial we get Friday Night Football rolling again at Herman Osteen Field," I told the two administrators.

Crowds currently were quite large for our small stadium; however, now we needed some of those young men in attendance to join us on the field to eventually take it to another level. During the dead period, I was able to explore current policies and communicate with other athletic programs in the event I oversaw the football program. My biggest sales pitch would target the baseball program to get them to buy in to shared athletes.

My interview was on a Wednesday, and it was a good one. As I explained my ambition and future goals for the program, Dr. Setterlund said something I would never forget.

"Often, Mike, the guy right after the long-term preacher that retires sometimes has the hardest task filling those shoes. Beyond that, the future and opportunity for change is wide open."

As the interview ended, I had a good feeling I had the inside track. I felt like I had now been there long enough to get a sense of the Collierville football tradition but could also choose a new direction for the future. I knew it wasn't going to be easy to sell an existing coaching staff the idea of an offensive rescheme that would no doubt ruffle some feathers; at the same time, I did have a plan to improve the facilities. Hopefully, in due time, another high school would be constructed, and we could start from scratch. At some point, we had to attract kids to the football program and keep the current ones playing here for the long haul.

The football banquet was on a Monday, December 4, and the hard work of planning this event was about to pay off. Again, coming off a dismal season, something had to end on a high note. No matter who became head coach, the off-season weight program would start the following week and the march toward the 2012 season would begin. That is how football works. It's a year-long process, especially when there is a change of the guard.

On banquet night I wore two hats: coach and dad. On a personal level, I was happy to see Michael elected by his peers and coaches as a Lifetime Team Captain for the season. He also made the Liberty Bowl All State Team. This is an annual all-star game for seniors played one week after the state championship game. He was the only one selected from Collierville; however, he suffered a concussion the Wednesday before the contest and was not able to participate.

While sitting at the head table, I glanced over my notes to ensure I wasn't leaving anything out or not thanking a group or spirit squads for supporting Dragon Nation. Tonight's speaker was a former Alabama football player and friend, Troy Secrest. He gave an excellent speech on setting goals, overachieving, and the drive required to make things happen. This guy was someone who had never played a down of football in high school, walked on at Alabama, and became a scholarship player by his senior year. Great story! As he spoke, I thought this was a perfect message for these seniors about to graduate.

Late in the program, Scott Hendrix walked up to the podium to wraps things up.

"Coach, we have added one more item to the program if that's okay?"

"Sure," I responded.

"I just received a note from Dr. Setterlund, and he would like to say a couple of words. Dr. Setterlund, the stage is yours," announced Scott.

As he walked up to the stage, I wasn't sure what he was going to do. I thought he might address the adversity we endured this season and maybe close out with some encouraging words for the future and brighter days ahead. Boy was I wrong!

"Gentlemen, I'm not going to lie or sugarcoat it. This season was beyond disappointing; some of you made some extremely bad decisions.

I hope you can learn from what happened, and quite frankly, some of your attitudes need to change immediately. Your future depends on it."

Doc didn't pull any punches and was to the point. It was a very somber moment as the players took a minute to reflect on their behavior and how they mismanaged their senior year. This message was harsh but needed to be heard. Then, after a couple minutes of silence and reflection, he continued.

"Okay, everyone, we will end this night on a positive note. After a month-long search, I would like to announce who your next Collierville Dragon head coach is…"

By this time, I was frozen in my seat, and I didn't have a clue if it were me or an outsider. I looked out, found Beth, and locked eyes with hers as my heart skipped a beat.

"Your new football coach will be your current interim coach and defensive coordinator—Coach Mike O'Neill!" Beth's face lit up. "Congratulations, Coach O'Neill!"

Unbelievable! I had no idea an announcement would come as soon as the banquet. I was elated and went back to the podium to join Doc. As I was collecting my thoughts, the applause was overwhelming.

"Thank you, Dr. Setterlund. Thank you, administration and Dragon Nation, for this opportunity," I said as I looked out into the banquet hall.

Obviously, nothing was planned, so I spoke from the heart in the attempt to express my gratitude and truly end the night on an upbeat note. For a period of five or so minutes, I shared my vision and goals.

"Men, we don't have a second to waste in getting ready for the 2012 season. Next week, we begin the off-season, so bring your A game!"

It was a wonderful night for the O'Neill family, personally and professionally.

CHAPTER 25

CHANGE IS NOT EASY

O VER THE PAST two years, our team strength was making gains, but speed and lateral movement had to improve. Plenty of teams in our league were bigger. We had to be stronger and more explosive in order to compete on Friday nights. Our program was designed so players could see their improvements on the board after every test in different categories. Good or bad, those numbers were going up. If guys were getting after it and eating right with proper recovery, significant gains happened. Testing day was energetic and rewarded players.

The repositioning of the coaching staff was going to change almost immediately. I had to look and evaluate our current staff. I knew this wasn't going to be easy, nor would I be the most popular guy around.

The assistant coaches at Collierville were all teachers first with six to seven classes and most had been here for fifteen-plus years. Three of the current assistants had been here more than twenty-five years. Bringing on new coaches was extremely hard, and it took three years before I could hire my first coach outside of the program. The problem was that if the assistant didn't teach a certain subject, then too bad, find someone who does. This approach was very similar in which CBHS operated as well. Coach Locastro over time had to start hiring non-faculty coaches to fill his staff.

There was nothing wrong with non-faculty guys; however, you had to find someone who worked at night, was self-employed and made their own hours, or an individual who was loaded with unlimited free time. It was certainly a challenge. In my mind, there was nothing like having a staff full of coaches who work in your school building and hold the student athletes accountable throughout the school day.

As time went on, I was able to persuade and motivate ex-Collierville players to help with the lower school programs and eventually the freshman team. I brought on a couple ex-players on the varsity staff over time, and they did an excellent job. Non-faculty coaches needed to be creative with their day jobs in order to pull it off. I understood the struggle because I did the same in my late teens and twenties to be a part of the middle school program at Germantown. What I liked about ex-players volunteering to assist the program was the loyalty they provided, not to mention their energy and willingness to learn ball.

However, my immediate task in my first year as head coach was to interview each assistant individually and attempt to gauge their expertise. I knew this wasn't going to be easy, and I was spot on. After the interviews, I moved forward in committing to a high-tempo zone read system with a single or two back look. Over the years, I have faced many zone read teams defensively and felt like with our lack of size and fullback/tight end types in the school building, my plan was simply to eliminate those two positions. The offence was to focus on zone reads and attack the perimeter of the defense. I certainly wanted an inside running game but knew our lack of offensive linemen could be a challenge to maintain a consistent attack inside the tackles.

Over the interview process, most of our staff was familiar with the flex bone offense that was used for many years at Collierville, but a couple young coaches who Coach Abel brought on board last year really captured my attention.

On the last day of the interview process, Josh Omura and Jonathan Abel came into the empty weight room coach's office to begin their presentation.

"Coach O'Neill," Jonathan spoke up, "Coach Omura and I heard the rumor you are leaning towards a run pass option, high-tempo offense?"

"Yes, news travels quick," I said.

Jonathan continued, "Coach, we are both here because we are coming from a co-coordinator's perspective. If granted the opportunity, I will handle the QBs and passing concepts."

"And I will handle the offensive line and running backs. Essentially, the run-game coordinator," Josh said.

"I'm listening."

Jonathan added, "Our QBs need to be smart, athletic, and willing to run the football based on the run-pass option concepts. If the defense loads the box and attempts to lock us up in man coverage all night, he must make plays in the passing game to pull defenders back out."

"We take what the defense gives us," Josh added.

"Everything is signal based; I will be on the sidelines and Coach Omura in the press box. With undersize offensive linemen, it's perfect because we can zone block and read a specific defender. Our guys need to be in great shape to pull it off, but we think it will happen based on our current personnel," Jonathan said.

As the interview continued, the inside run scheme was explained in full detail with opportunities to attack the perimeter of the defense with zone sweeps and short passing concepts. Everything was signal based and designed to limit substitution on the defensive side.

As the conversation was close to the end, they reminded me where they played together in college and who the head coach was. Yes, as they were presenting, I quickly gathered their angle. They played at

Lambeth University and their head coach was Hugh Freeze, who was, at the time, the head coach and offensive coordinator at the University of Mississippi. Jonathan was a receiver, and Josh was the center under Coach Freeze for four years at Lambeth, and both young men understood this offense like the back of their hands. Furthermore, Josh informed me two ex-Lambeth players are now graduate assistants under Coach Freeze at Ole Miss.

"We have access for anything we need in terms of film and information we desire for new concepts that come along."

I'd heard enough. These two were smart and experienced with this offense and the players loved them. Furthermore, the track record of Hugh Freeze and his success on the offensive side of the ball was undeniably effective, but having access to film cut ups and direct conversation with the Ole Miss offensive staff sold me.

The next day was extremely important. I brought in most of the staff who weren't coaching another sport to the Paul Cox Center to discuss and inform them of their new assignments. I anticipated the possibility that not everyone would be on board with this plan because most of the staff was under the Cox regime over the past several years and introducing a completely different concept would not be popular. Change can be tough to digest. I also made the decision to elevate two freshman coaches to the varsity staff and understood in due time I needed to backfill their roles and rebuild the ninth-grade staff over the off-season.

Pulling into the parking lot, I noticed most everyone had arrived. Upon entering the weight room, I sensed anxiety and now was absolutely convinced that everyone was anticipating possible changes. By the looks of things, an earlier meeting was quickly adjourned as I opened the door. At that time, the two offensive coordinators were making their way in from the parking lot. It was clear the three of us were not invited to the first meeting. *This first staff meeting is going to be a blast and there's no telling who's going to accept change or who might walk out and not coach next season.* I wasted no time getting down to business.

"Coaches, I appreciate you coming here on rather short notice, and I know there is an element of angst moving forward based on our individual meetings."

You could hear a pin drop. After, I proposed my philosophy and goals for the program for the immediate and long-term future, I directly addressed the elephant in the room.

"Gentlemen, next season, we will look completely different offensively with a new doctrine of thought. First, we are converting to a run-pass option system that will incorporate a zone-blocking scheme in a one or two back set that will operate at an extremely high tempo. The offense is designed to get the defense on their heels with limited ability of defensive personnel adjustments. It's no secret, with the lack of offensive linemen, the running game will have an option to pass on the table most downs. The QB will be taught to recognize pre-snap about numbers in the box or if the defense is tilted to one side. After the ball is snapped, the QB will be responsible for reading a designated defender in the box to determine the opportunity to hand off or keep the football. The offensive linemen must communicate with one another to adjust, and our receivers *must* learn to block and run excellent routes every down. Essentially, the QB is another potential running back; however, he will be required to make plays in the passing game. He must be smart, athletic, and extremely tough. Alex Hicks is our guy. He can do it. This year, I have selected two coaches to run this system by using a dual coordination approach. Coach Abel will run our passing game and coach up the QBs; Coach Omura will coach the offensive line and running game. I will add a pair of coaches to help with receivers and running backs."

Yes, this was bold, but I could only hope our existing staff would buy in from the start, because we had a ton of work to do in preparing all staff and players with a new philosophy, playbook, and signals. I made the decision to kick back spring practice to May, so we could have a couple months to learn the system.

The body language and lack of response indicated this change was not being received well.

"Some of you will coach new positions, and some of you will switch to the other side of the ball from last season, so I need you to buy in and give it your best shot, men. I realize change is not easy; however, I'm asking you to trust me."

After the announcement was made, the guys hit the ground running. We knew we needed to install a signal-based offense immediately at Collierville High School. Also, we needed to get this done before spring practice in May. Almost daily, these guys taught the system to prospective offensive players, and the kids loved it. They were taught the fundamentals and the potential opportunities a run-pass option offense could generate at 100 mph. It was drilled in their minds: "Every time we get the football, score and go score again!" Over the next few months, these guys did an excellent job teaching the offense to other assistant coaches and our players.

One day, after a weight room and chalk talk session, Jonathan asked me if we could meet in privacy about a personal dilemma. I could sense his concern by the distraught look on his face.

"Come on, let's meet right now, Jonathan," I said as I closed the office door.

"Coach O'Neill, I have an opportunity to coach at an Ivy League school next season," Jonathan said as I sat there speechless.

He continued, "Right after the end of last season, I applied to several schools for a coaching position, obviously prior to me accepting the OC job here at Collierville. One reached out yesterday. They want me to fly up next week to interview for an offensive position coach. I wanted to talk to you before I entertain the prospect of interviewing for the job."

After a brief pause, I said, "Jonathan, what are your coaching goals? What is your ambition?"

"Coach O'Neill, I want to get into football at the collegiate level at some point; however, I know this opportunity to coordinate at my 6A alma mater at my age was a unique situation. I'm at a loss to even think of going through the interview process. I just wanted to be upfront and get your honest opinion."

"Coach Abel, you have a very important decision to make, and I totally will understand if you move forward to go through with the interview. Personally, I would be shocked if you didn't go through with it based on the opportunity. I will back whatever decision you make."

Obviously, I wanted him to stay at Collierville, but I wasn't going to talk him out of a dream he had set in motion some time ago.

After two weeks of phone interviews, one in-person meeting, and hours of exploring his new opportunity, Jonathan decided to pursue coaching at this prestigious institution, and I supported and encouraged him to give it 100 percent of his attention. His efforts resulted in him landing the job.

Now, something needed to be altered moving forward with the offense now that we had one coordinator instead of a dual scenario. I just lost the passing game coordinator part of the job along with the QB coach. So, back to the drawing board with Josh to ensure his capabilities of handing both. As we discussed passing concepts within this run-pass offense system, he simply sold me on the idea to continue and move forward with this offense under his leadership. We had almost invested four months of work in teaching blocking and passing schemes, and spring practice was a short two weeks away.

With hours of further discussion and board talk, I was convinced he could handle it. Coach Omura would lead our offense going into my first season as head coach. Now, to give him help on offense, I had to adjust some of the staff who originally was going to help on defense. Everyone who was helping that off-season was thrown in the fire that spring. We had a few other coaches involved with winter and spring sports, so I switched them to the defensive side of the ball to give them the summer to polish up on defensive schemes and fundamentals. I knew our staff and players needed as much time developing this new offense along with signals and their own vocabulary before the first game in August. There wasn't a second to spare! So, before we ever stepped on the field for spring practice, tons of work had to be done in building strength and speed while learning a new offensive philosophy that included running a play every seventeen seconds. With all the effort and change happening within our program, the football team and the entire Collierville community was about to get a life lesson on how precious life truly is.

CHAPTER 26

LIFE IS SO PRECIOUS

THE BUILDUP TO spring practice was well underway. We agreed mid-May was time so we could include other athletes from winter sports and perhaps some track and JV baseball players when their season was completed. Also, I wanted to do it late so we could teach and digest this new high-tempo offense. Furthermore, we sprinkled in a new twist for a spring game to keep our new offense under the radar as much as possible. In order to get as many reps as possible, we decided to have an intrasquad game with TSSAA referees. My plan was to hype it school wide to get people excited about our new look before the season started in a couple short months. In the process, we were able to use everyone in the scrimmage and had a great crowd.

During the off-season workouts, our program and community was hit with some catastrophic news about one of our rising junior football players, Trey Erwin.

I received a phone call from Lisa (Trey's mom) saying Trey had been injured in a recreational basketball game with a potential bruise to his abdomen area.

"The doctor explained to Jay and me that Trey needs more tests to evaluate potential internal bleeding or possible other injuries Trey might have sustained during that basketball game," Lisa described.

By the sound of her voice, I could sense she was feeling something far worse was happening to her oldest son.

That next Sunday afternoon, Beth handed me my cell phone.

"You missed a call. It was Lisa Erwin."

"Yes. She's probably calling with the test results." I went on to explain what I currently understood about his injury and what was known thus far. "His name is Trey, a sophomore receiver. We call him Bieber."

"Bieber?" she asked with a puzzled look on her face.

"Justin Bieber. He looks just like him. Same hair and everything," I explained with a giggle. "Great kid. They live just around the corner in the neighborhood," I added.

I started dialing their number. "Lisa, Mike O'Neill, how are you?" I could hear sobbing on the other end.

"What's wrong?" Beth whispered as I held up a finger.

"Mike, Trey has pancreatic cancer," she said between sobs.

I shut my eyes…

"What is it? What is it?" Beth asked, tapping me on the arm.

I immediately put the phone up so Beth could now hear Lisa's voice.

"Yes, the doctors were suspicious of cancer from his bloodwork last week; however, we had to wait on a pet scan this week to confirm it." There was more crying on her end.

I looked at Beth, and now tears were rolling down her face as I was speechless.

"Coach, he might have four to six months left to live. It's stage four without a known cure."

I hardly could believe what I was hearing. As the sad conversation ended, Beth and I stood there crying while holding one another.

CHAPTER 27

#13 & #32

WITHIN A SHORT period of time, our football program and the entire Collierville community were beyond devastated when they heard that Trey Erwin had stage four pancreatic cancer. *What?* I remember thinking. *How does a fifteen-year old have pancreatic cancer? This is like a middle-aged person disease, right?* There were more tests performed, and then eventually treatment began at St. Jude Children's Hospital in Memphis. This news was hard to digest. I couldn't believe it! He was just in the weight room before that basketball game, and he hadn't missed one day. Trey was an extremely hardworking kid, but going back and looking at his weight chart, he had lost a decent amount of weight during that winter workout season.

Like everyone in our school community, my heart was hurting for him and his family because of what was ahead. The cancer had traveled to his liver and other organs, and ultimately the current treatment was to slow down the inevitable, with very little chance of curing it. Beth and I were so sad; it was overwhelming.

After word got out about Trey's condition, it didn't take long for regional media to take off with it. Overall, they did some incredible, uplifting stories about Trey's battle with his terminal condition. Trey was a complete warrior through the process, and he kept his faith through his battle. His journey has certainly aided my attitude in my current situation.

Upon receiving his terrible news, I gave the boys a couple weeks to digest what had happened. Upon returning from spring break, the team dedicated their efforts moving forward to Trey Erwin. During the spring game in May, Trey was rejuvenated and joined us as the team captain and spent the entire game on the sideline. Prior to that, I would take the squad on team runs to Trey's house, about one-and-a-half miles from the football training facilities, to spend some time with their teammate. Most days, he would make it downstairs for a quick talk and team prayer, but it was just heart-wrenching to see the weight loss and the unbelievable struggle Trey was enduring. Looking back, those runs were hard, but it made a strong connection between Trey and his teammates, and that was positive for everyone! I wanted to keep it real for them, and everyone had a chance to witness his struggles and an opportunity to pray for him and his family during their difficult time. We wanted him to know he was not alone in his battle.

As school let out for summer, Trey's condition continued to diminish. During the TSSAA mandatory off-period, Trey passed away on July 5 with his family by his side.

While on a beautiful sunny beach in Destin, Florida, on family vacation, I looked at my cell as Lisa Erwin's name popped up. My heart jumped because I knew what I was about to hear.

"Mike, Trey passed away peacefully this morning."

The beautiful surroundings of the emerald coast immediately turned murky and gray.

"Jay and I would like you to speak on behalf of the Collierville High School community and football family about Trey at his funeral in a few days," Lisa said.

I brushed away tears with back of my sandy hand. "I would be honored, Lisa."

Beth and I packed up immediately and began the journey home. I tried to persuade her to stay with the kids and I'd fly back for the funeral.

"No, we need to be together as a family during this time. It's very important we do this."

Beth was always right when we got into crisis mode. She invariably would see the entire picture of various situations and always made the right decision come crunch time.

On the drive home, I was able gather my thoughts about what I wanted to share about Trey. While the kids were in the back of the SUV asleep or watching videos, my thoughts turned to another former player who had passed away entirely too soon in life, whom I was extremely close to. The remembrance of his passing and the impact this young man had on his family, friends, and school community gave me the strength, motivation, and calm demeanor to see it through. His name was Chris Mosby.

Chris Mosby was a three-year all-state linebacker and team captain the year Christian Brothers High School played for the state championship in 2005. Not only was he a great player and heavily recruited, but he was that person who everyone looked up to for leadership and guidance. Chris was a generational athlete coming out of St. Louis Junior High in the Memphis area and was a four-year starter on the varsity football team, which was a rare accomplishment at the large division level. I honestly believe when he was in eighth grade, he could have played significant minutes on varsity.

As the defensive coordinator, my relationship with Chris over the years only grew stronger over time. By his junior year, Chris made every on-field adjustment on defense from his middle linebacker position. His football IQ was one of the best I have ever witnessed. It was almost impossible to find a player so talented and who understood the game so well. He was like having a coach on the field, which made my job that much easier. His senior year, we were ranked number one in the state for overall defense, points allowed, sacks, turnover ratios— you name it. Above all, Chris was one of those rare high school kids who made it feel like you were having a conversation with a twenty-something-year old and just a good person. Over time, we developed an incredible coach-player relationship, and I knew how special this young man was and couldn't wait to see his future unfold. About a week after the state championship, he verbally committed to Kentucky to play college football. The future was beyond bright for Chris.

About a month after the state championship game on the morning of December 31 at 6:00 a.m., while on a family winter vacation in the foothills of North Carolina, I received a phone call from a sad Kevin Locastro.

"Mike, sorry to call you so early, but I wanted to share some very sad news. Chris Mosby died in a one-car accident in Memphis just after midnight only a few hours ago."

This was utterly the saddest news I had ever received at that point of my life. How could this be? Why did this happen? How could his parents go through something like this? I felt like a member of my family had just died! The entire Christian Brothers community was in complete shock, which lasted the entire spring semester. Chris was the heart and soul of the school and was friends with almost everyone who met him. This young man was loved by everyone.

That spring after the passing of Chris, I was able to obtain approval from the school and family to develop a three-on-three basketball tournament in Chris's honor. It was run by my business classes to raise money for a scholarship fund and a sizeable donation to St. Jude's Children Hospital in Chris's name. The Chris Mosby 3v3 Spring Classic was a class project developed and managed by students to run a school-wide three-on-three basketball tournament played the first week in April. The six classes were broken down like a corporate business and each class had executives, operations, sales, and marketing. We had a team of student financial specialists who would report to the controller before and during the tournament for proper checks and balances. Revenue was generated by team sales, concessions, T-shirts, and corporate donations. Overall, the tournament ran for seven years and raised an average of $20,000 per year on the first Saturday in April. The main purpose of this tournament was to keep the memory of Chris Mosby going in the Christian Brothers community. The tournament eventually evolved with music and dunk tanks that teachers signed up for.

Through that experience, the passing of Chris Mosby prepared me to handle Trey's death with strength and the goal of keeping Trey's memory going. Today Collierville has the "Erwin Award," which is Collierville's version of the Heisman, and the Trey Erwin Scholarship Fund goes to a player who had a fighting spirit along with an incredible attitude like Trey possessed. This scholarship was funded by Lisa and Jay Erwin. Current coach, Joe Rocconi, vowed to keep Trey's memory going in the future.

That off-season, my first year as head coach really taught me how good the Collierville community truly was and not to take anything or anyone for granted in this ever-changing world; #13 Trey Erwin and #32 Chris Mosby will live in my heart forever.

CHAPTER 28

THE REWARDS & CHALLENGES
OF BEING HBC

T HE YEAR 2012 was yet another year of professional challenge, but it also provided quite a bit of personal adaptation to our ever-busy lives. Beth and I were both taking on new challenges and adjusting our lives; we now had two children at the University of Tennessee in Knoxville while our youngest, Mary Elizabeth, was enjoying her senior year at St. Agnes. Yes, I tried to talk her into joining me for her senior year at CHS, but she only entertained that thought for about fifteen minutes. It was also quickly vetoed by Mama O'Neill. My son started his freshman year at Tennessee, and Beth and I had to adjust to him being six hours away, just like we experienced with Brooke. We wanted to cherish Mary's last year as a senior and understood we would be empty nesters in the not-too-distant future. It wasn't going to be easy either. Falls were always the toughest because in late July, Beth turned into a football widow.

In the fall of 2012, time spent away from my family went to a whole other level. More head coaching responsibilities were heading in my direction, and we both knew the time demands were going to increase. Beth currently was experiencing that with her district manager role, which had her managing fifty team members. She understood it meant dealing with everyone's issues, good or bad. Professionally, she was already knee deep in a head coach role at the Sprint Corporation. My role would increase in the fall because of my responsibility of making sure every young man left the locker room every day safe and accounted for.

The 2012 off-season required an enormous amount of man hours in running the weight room four days a week, along with monthly booster club meetings, not to mention the time it required to install a brand-new offense. Again, the summer build-up to the season just intensified after the mandated mid-summer dead period, and it was pretty much that way since the banquet was complete in early December.

Seeing a child off for the first time is extremely hard, especially when you are on your own. I remember Beth coming back to Memphis on a Saturday night to the annual Bridge Builder Liberty Bowl game in 2006 after she took our oldest, Brooke, to college for her freshman year, and it was excruciating for her. The good news was that we won the game. The bad news was that Beth was as upset as I had ever seen her.

I walked over to the tunnel after the victory and looked up in the stands to see Beth's face. I was elated to see her, but I quickly noticed something was terribly wrong. As she came closer to the field, I could tell she had been crying and was visibly upset. "What's wrong?"

"I'll explain in the car," she replied as she continued to weep.

Later, I learned she cried the entire way from home from Knoxville, for nearly six hours straight.

It broke my heart she had to experience that farewell alone. It makes me sad every time I think about it. The next time we had a freshman go up, I was going to make 100 percent sure I was part of the journey.

The fall of 2012 was Michael's first at UT Knoxville and coming home was as painful as Beth had described. Now that I saw this first-hand, I couldn't imagine doing it alone. We had anticipated this year was going to be rough, and our expectations were right on, and I'm so glad I was there to share the emotion of having a child leave the nest. For me, spending all those years at school, on the practice fields, and games were incredibly special. All those years coaching his competitive baseball teams, spending weekend after weekend at tournaments, was extremely rewarding to both Beth and me. Beth was extremely close to Michael also because she went into labor at seventeen weeks, and he had RSV as an infant. He was almost three when he started sleeping in his own bed. He was just so small after birth, and with the RSV lasting over a year, we just didn't take any chances with him. The crib got moved into our bedroom and then he eventually moved into our bed. It's funny and often cute, but on occasion, his six-foot-two, 225 lbs. frame would plop down right in the middle of us to catch a show on cable, and before you knew it, it was the next morning. Beth and I never cared. So, when we dropped him off to college, it was brutal.

I clearly remember pulling out of the parking lot at Reese dorm. Beth and I dragged it out as long as possible with endless advice on multiple topics.

"Go to class, sit in the front, and get to know the professor on day one," Beth instructed.

"Okay, buddy. There is probably a party every night, so pick your battles. Have fun, but not too much," I chimed in. "Come on, sweetie, let's hit the road."

As we slowly drove off, Beth and I were overcome with tears as I saw Mike in the rear-view mirror grinning from ear to ear, giving us the thumbs-up! *Damn*, I thought, *the party and freedom is just beginning for young, Mikey.* And he knew it.

On the way back home to Collierville, I didn't have any time to wallow in misery as we made our way to Shelby County. That next week was game week, and I had to get my mind turned quickly on the task of being a head coach. Film and practice preparations were only a small part of it. I found out very quickly other head coaching responsibilities came in addition to my job as defensive coordinator.

That first season at Collierville, there was a huge learning curve with the logistics and challenges at our facilities. The coaches had new roles, a new offense, and a new leader. My first game as HBC, Beth invited friends and family from out of state to our first game with Hillcrest.

I looked across our immaculate game field and saw several friends and family sitting directly under the press box. *Man, we better win this game tonight,* I told myself.

As we took the field for pregame, a parent tried to get my attention. "Coach, the helicopter will be here on time to deliver the game ball."

"Thanks, Mr. Anderson. The pilot understands he needs to come in from the east, correct?"

That parent had organized a helicopter to bring in the game ball in honor of our fallen teammate, Trey Erwin, to kick off the season. That season, we rotated his game jersey (#13) for the player who had earned to wear it based on a great attitude and effort during that week of practice leading up to every game night. There was always a great competition to earn the right to wear the number 13 on Friday nights.

After my pregame speech, while huddled in the weight room, I announced it was "go time" as the steel bay door was pulled up by the chain harness.

"Let's take care of business, gentlemen," I said as we marched toward the south end zone to run through the Dragon tunnel. Everything that night went as planned to include my first victory as head coach for the Collierville Dragons.

That next off-season, the booster club was committed to expanding our feeder programs of full-contact football that the city of Collierville had abandoned a few years earlier. Plans to expand in the future were on the table. This was a huge undertaking; however, it was overdue. We interviewed, hired and conducted clinics for coaches to buy into our way of doing things. The old school days of Lombardi and Bryant were not working in today's suburban America. Kids now had multiple choices in the fall, including lacrosse, fall baseball, and club soccer, and many committed to being a one-sport athlete.

Football in Collierville had been dying since the mid-2000s, and the opportunity to expand to the lower grade schools was beyond critical. Eventually, we expanded to flag teams that would feed into the tackle leagues. At one point, our program had eleven teams in the system. The workload was extremely high, and we had to negotiate with the city to find practice facilities and game sites for every team.

In due time, our numbers and population started to expand in the lower school and middle school with the help of our booster club. The marketing efforts and visits to middle and elementary schools began to pay dividends, moving in the right direction.

Year in and year out, our kids worked hard and played their butts off. Rarely did we have a bad practice, and guys *never* threw in the towel. However, the lack of offensive linemen and depth seemed to be a recurring theme and I wasn't exactly sure how to fix it. At times, we thrived with skill kids and QBs, and some years we were linebacker and defensive lineman heavy. We just couldn't get our personnel built up on both sides with ample depth.

The 2016 season started out as expected with two decisive wins, but after a good Monday practice and JV victory, early Tuesday morning, I was informed of the unthinkable. Our school Athletic Director/ Assistant Principal informed me that one of our players was ineligible in the first two games of the season. *What? How could this be?* The player had failed a summer school requisite and simply slipped through the cracks.

That Tuesday was consumed by several meetings between counselors, administration, and eventually the superintendent. Everything was transparent. I'm rules guy first with zero secrets. After several meetings, and the hope of our player to have enough credits to qualify, I made the painful decision to self-report to the TSSAA for our player being ineligible once it was determined he did not have enough credits to elevate him to be a senior. We knew it would be a day or two until the TSSAA would decide about the first two non-region games. The game plan was to keep the news within the coaching staff and the ineligible player in order to keep the distractions down while we prepared for Friday night with the hope that the first two games would be counted as victories. Unfortunately, that was not the case. Not only was our player ineligible for the remainder of the season, but we also had to disqualify the first two non-conference games of the 2016 season.

I remember spending almost half the day in the administration area of the building and thinking, *no way this could be happening to our program.* By this time, the principal, two vice principals, and the athletic director were giving this issue their full attention.

Just after lunch, I received the devastating news that Thursday from a TSSAA representative that we would be required to forfeit our first two contests of the season. I knew this was going to be gut-wrenching news for everyone in the program; however, it was imperative to level with the players before they left that day. I couldn't keep it from them anymore because of the different rumors flying around about the ineligible teammate who was not practicing with them.

After practice, I summoned the players on the fifty-yard line of the game field. "Guys, over the past few days, I have kept you in the dark, and I apologize. However, I just needed more information before making this unfortunate announcement."

As I looked into the eyes of ninety players, I knew this was not going to be accepted well.

"Men, we broke a rule with an internal oversight. It was discovered earlier this week that one of our players was academically ineligible for the first two games, and I made the decision to self-report the mistake the day it was discovered, with the hope the TSSAA would allow the two non-conference games to count as wins for the season."

The looks on their faces were of complete disappointment and disgust. "Unfortunately, the TSSAA came back with a decision and demand we forfeit those two games of the season. I'm sorry this happened."

It was not an easy conversation, and there was major disappointment. It was almost like the air suddenly dissipated. The seniors called for a closed meeting to discuss what they had just learned. They immediately took off to the north end zone to convene.

After the team regathered at midfield, one of the team captains spoke up to address the entire squad. "Guys, we have a choice. We can throw in the towel now, and be average the rest of the season, or we can play our asses off and make the best of it. We have started off great with an unfortunate situation, but this team had a great off-season, an incredible start to the season, and we are mentally tough. I say we fight like hell."

The captain made a great speech and the team bought in. He was correct. This team was mentally very tough; however, we didn't have time for any more distractions because our schedule was about to get brutal very quick.

That Friday, we lost to a very good White Station team in a close contest. As the season continued, we won big the next Friday, then went through three straight district losses, with two of them very close and lost in the final minutes of the game. Fortunately, we did well enough to squeeze a postseason berth and a decisive victory in round one over Wilson Central on the road. The following week, we narrowly lost to an 11-0 Cordova team deep into the fourth quarter. *These guys never quit.*

In the ensuing off-season, proper adjustments were made internally, and all head coaches now had access to all grades throughout the year. In the past, coaches had limited access to kids in summer school and others that went off the athletic study hall rosters. Checks and balances were also put into place to ensure kids were 100 percent eligible on the roster, and if not, they were left off until those requirements were met. Moving forward, this system allowed the head coach to access and not rely on the athletic director to finalize the eligibility report. It was explained that's how it was always done, but I demanded it to be changed by the next season.

This was an extremely tough lesson, but the decision not to report the incident to the TSSAA was not an option. I'm a rules person, and that option was never considered. In my book, integrity is everything!

CHAPTER 29

LEADING UP TO THE DIAGNOSIS

BETH KEPT A low profile but was extremely supportive. She had witnessed every uncomfortable scenario from negative press to an upset parent who showed up at our front door to discuss his son's game time at ten p.m. on a Sunday night. Beth was not only appalled, but somewhat frightened.

I had just settled into bed and turned on the late news while Beth was enjoying a bath to unwind after an active day of running around when the doorbell rang.

"Is that the doorbell?" she bellowed out from the confines of the bathroom.

By that time, I was marching to the foyer and saw a silhouette of someone standing through the door window on the unlit porch. It appeared to be a male. I turned on the porchlight and immediately recognized the parent of a player who happened to live in my neighborhood. I was thrown off guard and completely perplexed.

"Who is it?" Beth yelled from the bathroom.

I unlocked the metal storm door and slowly opened it. "Mr. Hollingsworth, everything okay? It's a bit—"

"We need to talk," he interrupted.

I knew this wasn't going to be your typical friendly neighbor chat. "Beth, Mr. Hollingsworth from around the corner is here. His son, Jesse, is a senior football player," I said, attempting to provide Beth some information before she promptly called the Collierville Police Department.

"Come in, Mark. Let's go to the back patio and talk," I said as I guided him to the patio. I could smell the alcohol on his breath.

After we took a seat at the patio table, he wanted to understand why his son was not getting any playing time on Friday nights.

Looking back, this parent was rather intoxicated and very unreasonable until I invited him in; then, I was able to talk him down. I guess he walked over because I didn't see a car. Beth was mortified and made me promise that I would not invite anyone else in who showed up unexpectedly at that time of night. I agreed.

One thing is for sure, Beth was outstanding about keeping me oblivious to the outside drama until Saturday. Throughout the week, Beth would get calls, texts, or emails sometimes that weren't urgent and put it off until Saturday evening—after our game film was evaluated late Friday night and after opponent film was broken down for the next week all day Saturday. Like clockwork, Saturday evenings we would sit down at the kitchen table and talk about events not football related.

"Okay, you ready for some non-football issues that need your attention?" she asked as she opened her notebook of items that needed to be discussed.

She was great about keeping me in the dark about something until Friday night had come and gone. Beth protected the distractions that could derail my football preparation. It certainly made my job easier, and I will always be grateful for her.

After getting settled back into our July pattern, we were going a

100 mph preparing for football camp. The third week of July, we were allowed helmets to acclimate our players to the eventual full pads in conditions that hover around one hundred degrees. That morning of the first day of helmet practice, I began to feel a twinge in my throat; however, this time it came back with more intensity and a bit more pain. *I thought I lost that uncomfortable feeling somewhere in the Pacific Ocean between Maui and the Big Island while on vacation.* I was wrong. It was basically in the same area, the right side of the back of my throat, with more intense pain.

After practice, I scheduled a visit to my primary doctor's office, and they indicated they could see me immediately if I could arrive in the next thirty minutes. Beth, who was now in Europe on business, insisted I get it checked out, so I popped in for an evaluation. Upon arrival, I met with a nurse practitioner and received a thorough evaluation and brief discussion about my strange throat pain. In short, I went through the entire gamut: vitals, bloodwork, and flu/strep test. The practitioner could not detect anything; however, I was given a prescription to be on the safe side and was instructed to gargle with warm salt water to reduce the pain.

"If this doesn't clear up in a week, I strongly suggest scheduling a visit with an Ear, Nose, and Throat doctor immediately," the nurse practitioner said.

After I left, I knew football would turn into two-a-days next week and decided to call my ENT doctor. They told me they didn't have any openings for two and a half weeks but would set the appointment.

That day I began taking my prescription and gargling with warm salt water, and after a couple days began to feel much better. Two more days went by, and I felt 100 percent and assumed my antibiotics were kicking in. I felt it would just be a burden to squeeze in a doctor's visit between practice and in-service before the kids would arrive the following week. I convinced myself I needed to cancel my doctor's appointment with the ENT, and that's precisely what I did.

Three weeks went by, and more pain came and went. Beth had

returned from her international trip, and I informed her I was going to get a mononucleosis test and bloodwork for tonsillitis. I dropped into a walk-in clinic on a Sunday to get tested, and both were negative. The nurse then provided stronger antibiotics with the hope of knocking out whatever could be causing this pain. Now minor swelling in my throat was apparent, but I still was not overly concerned.

Through the busy season, and frankly our busy lives, I called back the ENT, and he insisted that I come in immediately. This time I went to see a doctor. They scheduled me a couple weeks out, and my appointment was in the second week of October to get a closer look and hopefully some answers.

On our bye week, Beth and I went to Pittsburgh for a family wedding, and by that time, the pain was getting downright uncomfortable. Now I could feel the growth in the back of my throat, and Beth determined a lymph node in my neck was swollen. My appointment was on the following Monday, and I could hardly wait. I had convinced myself I had some type of tonsillitis, and I would have to get them removed. Perhaps I could wait until the season was done.

That Monday came, and Beth and I went to see Dr. Turner. Dr. Turner has been a long-time doctor of Beth and removed Michael's tonsils a couple years ago. Dr. Turner opened the door and quickly went to work.

"Mike, at this point, we need to biopsy this area today, because we need some answers soon. The antibiotics are not working, so we need to rule out some things before we move forward."

What things? Now my mind was racing. I looked at Beth and she had a concerned look on her beautiful face. I now started to worry.

"Let's take a look," he said as he peered into the back of my throat.

I opened my mouth to maximum capacity, and he administered a shot of numbing medication in my right tonsil area. "Let's give it about five minutes," he said.

"Doctor, could this be cancer?" Beth asked.

He looked down. "I'm afraid so. The results from the biopsy next week and the X-ray in about fifteen minutes will provide a much clearer picture."

"Any chance it's an infection or tonsillitis?" I said as I attempted to cancel out the C word.

"Yes, to the infection, unlikely to tonsillitis. Both tonsils would be impacted. In your case, only one is inflamed." He then picked up a needle attached to a syringe to extract tissue from the inflamed area.

"This shouldn't hurt a bit," he said as he plucked out five or six tissue specimens. I only felt a slight nip as he was extracting multiple samples. He then left the room after the biopsy was complete.

Beth softly spoke up, "I was afraid of this Mike."

"What? No way. This must be an infection or maybe one tonsil needs to come out. He said there was a chance."

Beth interrupted, "A small chance."

After about five minutes of silence and deep thought, Dr. Turner returned and indicated the results would take about a week and pointed me down the hall to the area to get the X-ray.

Twenty minutes later, we all met back in the examination room. Dr. Turner said we would meet next week to discuss the results.

"Doctor, before we leave, would you mind if I take a pic with my cell phone of the X-ray?" Beth politely asked.

"Sure."

Beth snapped four pictures.

We soon left the office without a word.

CHAPTER 30

THE WEEK THAT CHANGED EVERYTHING

THAT MONDAY MORNING trip to the ENT for a biopsy was followed with three hours of business classes, football practice, and a JV game that night. However, this week was a bit more intense. Not only because of my health, but because it was Houston game week. The Houston Mustangs and the Collierville Dragons are archrivals. To say it is intense would be a major understatement! Every year, rain, snow, or excessive heat, the stadium is packed. Even kids who don't care for football or sports in general that much will ask me in the classroom, "Coach, are we going to beat Houston this year?"

It was intense because our communities overlapped, and some students who lived in Collierville went to Houston High School in nearby Germantown before the schools went to municipalities school districts. Still, they privileged some of these kids in because they gave them the option to choose a school while they were in junior high. So, some of those students (football players) who lived in the common areas could choose which high school to attend for a period of four years. Those kids were now seniors. So, let the smack talk begin.

From year-to-year players, coaches, and students remember the score from the previous season, talk smack, and predict the winner. This year it was as heated as ever. Both schools were doing well at 5-3 and positioning for a home-field advantage in the playoffs. We were coming off a four-game winning streak and playing good football. Houston had won the past four out of five contests, and a victory would determine state playoff seeds in the coming weeks. However, this one came down to school pride. Guaranteed, 90 percent of the people in the stadium at Herman Osteen didn't give a flip about play-off seeds or home-field advantage; they just wanted bragging rights to their buddies and cross-county foes for the next 365 days. This was "Houston Week!"

That day was extremely long! I had an early doctor's appointment, class, practice, a JV game, more film watching, and bed around eleven thirty. I hadn't seen Beth since that morning and almost actually forgot about the doctor visit. When I returned home, she was asleep. The next morning was my usual: get up at five a.m. and out by six. As I kissed her goodbye before I left, she was on her phone and quiet and some-what distant. Maybe she was checking Facebook or Instagram; I didn't ask. That evening, after practice, we sat down for dinner, and now she was downright sad. I knew what was on her mind, and I reminded her that everything would be good.

I said, "Maybe I can have my tonsils out right after the season. You wait and see."

I could tell she was not buying what I was selling. She just told me to expect that this could be a lot worse than I thought. She continued to thumb through her phone. I could see she was sad, yet extremely determined.

Wednesday rolled around, and I continued to bury myself into work. It was A-game Wednesday, and we were having a great practice week. I would deal with my medical situation during the appointment next week when the results from the labs came back from the biopsy. He told me it would take at least a week, so my concentration and focus were on our critical game with Houston.

After another long practice, I told Beth and Mary that I would not join them at the Memphis Grizzlies game that was on the calendar for Beth to host clients downtown at the Forum. Usually I would go, but I just felt tired and worn out. I just wanted to watch some more game film and get plenty of rest for a huge game in a couple days.

It was about 6:45 p.m. when I arrived home after practice. "A-game Wednesday" was a phrase I would say every week to remind them that we need to get everything together before our walk-through on Thursdays. Wednesday, like every other day, was important, but it was critical that every assistant hammered out every detail or issue we may have in the game plan before we hit the locker room that evening. Thursdays were meant to fine-tune the game plan and not worry about unresolved issues. The hay needed to be in the barn by the end of practice on Wednesday. I felt good about this week; we had a sound game plan, and our squad was playing good football. This team was heading in the right direction, and now it was time to take it to our biggest rival and attempt to accomplish our regular season goal of hosting a round one playoff game for this season.

After a quick shower, I made some dinner and sat on the couch to watch something drama-free on TV. It'd been a busy week, and I was tired. As I began to eat my dinner, my cell phone rang. I didn't recognize the number, but that was the norm in my world. Often, I would get calls from a parent, the media, a player, or a college coach. My phone pretty much went off constantly day and night, and most numbers were not in my log.

"Hello?"

"Hello. Is this Ronald O'Neill?"

"Yes, this is Mike. Whom am I speaking with?"

"Dr. Turner."

My heart sank immediately. This was the potential news I was going to get on Monday of next week. I had already categorized that in my mind, and this was totally unexpected.

"Yes, sir. How can I help?"

"I need to tell you something very serious. Can you talk?"

My heart sank for a second time. "Yes, go ahead."

"Mike, I hate to give you this disappointing news, but you tested positive for squamous cell carcinoma in your right tonsil area."

A couple moments went by, and I said, "Wow, those results came back fast. What's the next step?"

"Mike, this is a very serious situation with a very intense treatment plan, but it's not a death sentence necessarily. However, your life is about to change dramatically."

About a thousand things at once were running through my mind; my major focus was on informing Beth and the rest of my immediate family. As we got off the phone, he said to keep our appointment open for Monday so we could discuss our options and potential treatments from different cancer hospitals.

"Start looking for an oncologist that specializes in throat and head/ neck cancer," he said.

As we hung up the phone, my entire body was completely numb.

My first thought was to call Beth. She and Mary were in a crowded, loud suite, and I wasn't sure if she would even answer. She picked up after the first ring and stepped out into the hallway adjacent to the luxury suite. As I told her about my conversation with Dr. Turner, she began to cry and reminded me that we will get through this together.

"Mary and I are coming home now."

I began calling my children, parents, and siblings. The calls were excruciating, and a long pause would follow from most of the recipients. For some strange reason, I remained calm and wasn't as upset as I thought I would be. It's hard to describe, but I was ready to fight my disease the minute I was informed I had it. Maybe it was a defense mechanism for what was going on deep inside. Even today writing about it, I can hardly believe my mindset when I originally heard the news.

My biggest fear was the inconvenience and worry I would put Beth, the kids, and my family through and endure because of my diagnosis. That was my biggest heartache, not personally anticipating what would happen to me, but the people who loved and cared for me. When I told my parents, it was extremely hard because my mom was fighting a terrible battle of her own and this was the last thing she needed to hear.

"Hey, Dad. Get Mom on the phone please. I have something important I need to share." I began to pace around the kitchen in attempt to calm my nerves.

"Hello, Michael. It's Mom. We are both on speaker."

"Mom, Dad, I'm not sure how to say this and I apologize for catching you off guard."

"What is it, Mike?" Dad asked.

"I have throat cancer, Dad." Silence echoed on their end.

While I continued to pace, I repeated my entire conversation with my doctor only minutes ago. This was the one phone call I dreaded the most. Then, my dad perked up. "Mike, you can beat this… Mike, did you hear me?… You *will* beat this!"

Just what I need to hear, I thought as I quit pacing the floor.

About the time I talked to my last immediate family member, Beth and Mary returned from downtown. Beth had been crying over the last hour, and it was downright the low point of the night. After they settled in, I informed them of my conversation with Dr. Turner. As I talked, I could tell Beth had a lot on her mind, and she wanted to share it.

Beth told me that we had this. "You will get admitted to MD Anderson or Vanderbilt, depending on who will take our insurance. If we choose MD Anderson, we can take off whenever."

"What? Slow down! What or how do you know all of this? I just found out the news about an hour ago. Have you been making a ton of calls since we spoke?"

I looked at Mary, and she just shrugged her shoulders and looked back at her mom.

"Okay Mike. I need to level with you," Beth proclaimed.

At that second, I could see that the tears were dry, and a plan was about to be introduced. I knew that look on my wife's face when her sheer determination kicked in. It was crisis mode, and she was already in fourth gear.

"What?" I asked.

"Mike," she said, "let me tell you about the last forty-eight hours. Now hear me out."

Okay, I thought. *I'm listening.*

She said, "As we left Dr. Turner's office on Monday, remember the picture I took of your X-ray?"

"Yes."

"Well, I started to do some research."

"Okay, I'm with you."

"I inquired to my friend Ginger about sending the picture of the X-ray to her brother, who is a radiation oncologist to see what his thoughts were just based on the X-ray of the growth in the back of your throat. So, I sent the photo to my friend, who sent it to her brother, who then informed Ginger that he was ninety-nine percent sure that this was squamous cell carcinoma in the throat and growing."

"What? Wait. Why didn't you tell me?" I exclaimed.

"I wanted you to hear the news directly from your doctor," she replied.

I was speechless. She then explained she was extremely sad over the last forty-eight hours but started the process of looking for different cancer centers in the U.S. for throat cancer. She had already reached out to them, but lab results and a doctor's recommendation were holding the process up. Now that it was confirmed, Dr. Turner had encouraged me only an hour ago to look at different options. He went on to suggest a throat cancer specialist. *Unbelievable,* I thought, *Beth got a serious jump on my cancer some forty-eight hours ago.* To be honest, it was not too surprising as that is how Beth O'Neill rolled. She didn't wait on things to happen; she made things happen! She also informed me that in the morning we would contact all of them, but MD Anderson was on the top of the list.

"Why?"

"Because they have a proton therapy unit at MDA," Beth insisted.

"Proton, what?"

"Proton therapy. It's a very small radiation beam that is ideal for head/neck cancer. It's designed with pinpoint accuracy to hit the bad cancer cells and leave the healthy cells alone."

She also informed me these proton centers were extremely rare around the world, and the only one in Memphis was at St. Jude Children's Research Hospital.

"However, you are way too old to qualify for that one at this point, so Houston and Nashville were our closest options."

Beth had researched three separate hospitals offering potentially three similar treatment options. Beth knew each hospital would have its pros and cons. MD Anderson was the furthest away, so living arrangements would need to be investigated if they took our insurance. Nashville was also an option being only three hours away, but would they accept our insurance. The West Clinic was in Memphis but didn't have proton therapy. Hopefully, by Friday, we could pinpoint our hospital and begin to make living arrangements. Wednesday night had a brief state of sadness, but now that had been replaced by task mode. Beth was now in her third day of researching what would be our best place to achieve maximum results. I just listened.

So many things were racing through my mind, now that we had concrete answers about my condition. *Is this a death sentence? Will the treatment involve surgery, radiation, and chemo? How long to recover? How long will I be away from friends and family?* That night we talked about all options.

Football was getting lower on the priority list; however, I knew nothing would change between now and Friday night. I didn't want my health to be a distraction. There were just too many coaches, players, and fans invested, so making an announcement prior to kickoff would not be an option. I spoke to my immediate family, and they honored my wishes by not saying a peep. At that time, I was up to the task, and I could keep my emotions in check. Furthermore, it was a damn good distraction from my current condition. I felt so run down and tired, but that announcement would be made post-game Friday: win, lose, or draw.

On Thursday, while I was teaching and preparing our team for Houston, Beth was calling each hospital admission department to finalize our plans. Vanderbilt came back first and denied our insurance. The West Clinic, at the time, had only one specialist who specialized in head/neck cancer, and our information was hung up in their system. In the meantime, MD Anderson in Houston informed Beth that a referral and current insurance were being examined that very moment to see if I could be approved for proton therapy. Most insurance companies will not insure this therapy because of the expense. Beth had researched proton therapy, and she was pushing extremely hard for me to get this treatment. She even reached out to the insurance company and was set up with a personal representative who pushed hard for approval.

Beth called first thing Friday to speak with an MDA representative, and the rep informed her that a decision had not yet been made at that time on my case. Beth was fearful her insurance would be denied or not accepted at MDA as well. At that moment, she asked God to help us get accepted to MD Anderson in Houston, Texas. Just then, right after the prayer, the MDA rep said, "Hey, we are in luck! Your insurance was just accepted!"

"Oh, my goodness," she replied.

"This never happens! I've never had a patient on the phone at the very moment that it's announced that they were admitted."

Beth started crying immediately and told the rep what had just happened. Beth explained to her that while on the phone early in the conversation, she was praying to God, Mary, and a host of saints for help, and they were listening. She went on to say after she explained this to the MDA rep, she could hear crying on the other end of the line.

That late Friday morning after my last class, I came home for a quick lunch before I headed back to the football complex. Beth informed me what had happened and said we are going to Houston for cancer treatment. At that very moment, I could feel the Holy Spirit working when she explained to me what had happened over the phone about an hour ago.

"When are we going? How long?" I eagerly asked.

"Not sure, but hopefully later today we will know."

I told Beth that either way, I was going to level with the coaches, players, and administration right after tonight's game, and she agreed. In the meantime, Michael was on his way from Nashville, and Brooke was making plans to come in for tonight's game.

As I went back to the coach's office to begin the game prep, Beth called to inform me our first appointment would be on October 31, a week from the upcoming Monday. At that moment, I decided not only to inform them of my condition after the game, but I would also explain that next Friday (senior night) would be my last game to coach this season because of my departure for Houston on the following Sunday. I also would tell the coaching staff of my decision for an interim coach and who would take over the defense upon my departure. There was a lot going through my mind, but I had to keep focused on tonight's critical game.

When the players began coming into the locker room, I put cancer aside for the next several hours. As pre-game neared and the Mustangs arrived, my thoughts about cancer and Houston, Texas, were lightyears away. Somehow, some way, I was able to bury everything for a three-hour period.

As the teams took the field for pre-game, I could see my family in the end zone supporting their husband, son, father, and G-Daddy (my chosen granddad name). It gave me the strength I would need to get through the night, and I knew 100 percent I wouldn't let my mind stray, not now with kickoff in thirty-five minutes. We had the Houston Mustangs in the house for senior night, and it was time to defend our turf.

When the game started, it was a typical Dragons vs. Mustangs contest, extremely close with multiple lead changes and emotions running high for players and fans. It was beyond full capacity in our undersized stadium. On paper we could hold about 2,300, but the gate receipts said there were twice as many who crammed in. I'm sure multiple fire codes were broken that night. Forget the playoff scenario or home-field advantage, these guys wanted Houston's ass and came out smoking with the early lead, but then fell by a touchdown in the second quarter; however, we then tied it up right before halftime.

The second half was the same, back and forth with several lead changes, but the Dragons took the lead late in the game with a two-point conversion. Houston started a drive at their twenty-five-yard line and scored a touchdown with no time remaining on the clock with the momentum completely in their favor. In short, Houston needed the two-point conversion to put the game into overtime with renewed vigor.

After the score, the Mustangs now huddled for the conversion almost before our guys could line up, so I called a time-out to reset. The moment I called the time-out, I noticed a fullback, tight end in their personnel packaging during the time-out, I told our guys to be ready for anything or any set, so I called two plays based on the personnel they chose to use.

As I jogged off the field after the completion of the time-out, Houston came out in an empty set as anticipated. Our guys quickly saw it and auto-checked to the RIP Mickey cover 0 and lined up fast to anticipate a quick count. RIP Mickey is a six-man blitz from a split-four look with defensive tackles lined up in two techniques (over the offensive guards) and the linebackers line up directly behind the defensive tackles. Pre-snap it is designed to cause confusion to the offensive linemen to pick up their blocks in a potential run or pass play.

As the Houston QB lined up in shotgun formation, our defense was locked and loaded. As the snap started, our two inside linebackers crisscrossed A-gap responsibilities. Thankfully, RIP Mickey caused complete confusion to the Houston offensive linemen. As the Mustang QB ran the draw, he simply acted like he was going to throw then took off up the gut. However, our blitzing linebackers caused complete mayhem in both A-gaps, which left our right defensive tackle untouched and provided a nice bear hug to the Houston QB at the one-yard line to win the game for the Collierville Dragons!

The whistle blew, and the Collierville side of the stadium unloaded onto the field. It was complete celebratory pandemonium with the field completely covered with fans, parents, and faculty. As the celebration continued, my mindset began to shift to the task at hand.

As I made my way to Houston's head coach and good friend, Will Hudgens, I told him great game and then whispered in his ear my recent diagnosis. He was clearly upset, and I told him to keep it under wraps until I could tell my guys in about ten minutes. Will was the first person who knew about my cancer outside of my family at that very moment.

While the mayhem continued, I began by gathering coaches to tell players to go to the football complex just beyond the track for a post-game meeting. At that time, I found two administrators and told them to find other administration and Principal Blanchard to gather in the weight room as quickly as they could find them. I was grabbing players and telling them in the middle of the chaos to get to the weight room now. Kids were looking at me like, "chill out, Coach, we just beat Houston." But I wanted to make sure they headed to the weight room before they took off uphill to the locker room. I just needed everyone there at the same time to deliver my message as a program.

Early in the week, I told my assistant coaches and Principal Blanchard that I went for a biopsy and anticipated the results the following week. As I continued to gather people in the weight room, administrators filed in, looking confused. Typically, they did not join in post-game speeches, and some told me later they thought I might have been upset with everyone storming the field post-game. Heck, they could have burned the place down, and I would have been oblivious to it at that point.

As players and coaches filed into the weight room, I saw my son, Michael, out of the corner of my eye. He came over and told me he loved me and said, "Dad, you will kick cancer's ass!"

That quick statement provided me the inner strength I needed for what was about to happen next. The players, coaches, and administration were now crammed into our 3,500 sq. ft. weight room.

"First, I wanted to congratulate everybody in our football program on a great week of practice. Tonight, you demonstrated that hard work and focus with a victory over the Houston Mustangs! Thank you for playing four quarters and never giving up, and that the last play of the game was indicative of that. Congrats again! We are guaranteed a playoff spot now!"

I paused.

"I want to change course of the conversation, and I don't mean to put a damper on a great night."

I paused again and took a deep breath.

"Coaches and administration, most of you guys know that I have been having pain in my throat the past couple months, and Monday I took a biopsy to determine what is causing my pain and the small knot that has formed in my right tonsil. I told some of you my results would come next week, and I would keep you posted. Well, the results came this past Wednesday. I held off until tonight to disclose what my doctors found until this game was over because I didn't want this to be a distraction or take away from the preparation towards this very important game tonight," I said before I took a sip of water and cleared my throat.

"I have throat cancer. Right now, it appears that I have squamous cell carcinoma, and that it probably started back in the summer."

Now you could hear a pin drop.

I looked into the eyes of the coaches and players, and the looks of sadness were overwhelming. We went from pure and utter elation to flat-out depression in a matter of two minutes.

"I'm sorry to tell you now on such a big night for our program, but I need to explain to you my treatment plan and timetable that will affect everyone in this room. Mr. Blanchard and administration, I will need some time off—weeks, maybe a few months. Coaches, I need you to take over in the not-too-distant future. Players, I need you to continue this momentum and help achieve our goals of the season."

The silence continued.

"Now, let me tell you how I'm going to fight and kick cancer's ass! I plan on going to MD Anderson Cancer Center in Houston, Texas, a week from Monday. Guys, I'm going to the top place in the world for throat cancer, but I can only coach you one more time this season. I will coach you next week, and at the conclusion of the game, I will get my mind on my cancer battle. Administrators, I will need a long-term sub probably up to five months, then I should be able to return by quarter four. That means spring practice for you football players. Guys, don't worry, I will overcome my diagnosis. I'm a man of faith, and I need your prayers, but I need everyone to finish extremely strong this season. You can go as far as you want this season. Go get a state championship!"

I took a breath and continued, "Coaches, I need you to support one another and be flexible with your responsibilities when I leave for Texas. After next week's game, I need to focus on my cancer battle and moving to Houston, Texas. I love everyone in this room, and please pray for my recovery. They say the treatment is intense, but I'm up for the battle. I'm going to freakin' embrace it!" I took a drink from my water bottle.

"So, enjoy tonight's big win, but tomorrow let's get all eyes on the Tigers from Arlington. Guys, I need this distraction of coaching football before I take off. At the same time, you must keep focused on the task at hand. I love you all."

I looked at our team Chaplin, Al Baker, and gave him the nod so he could bless our team. Our team FCA director asked everyone to gather around me and touch one another to bless this team, give thanks for protecting our players, and praying for my cancer recovery. You could hear crying as he said an incredible blessing.

At that very moment, Principal Blanchard got up on a bench-press bench and took a picture of the players surrounding me. I had one photo in my classroom and one in my exercise room at home. He captured that moment that ended one emotional week that would change everything for my family moving forward.

CHAPTER 31

10 PERCENT CHANCE OF RAIN

THAT NEXT MORNING came quickly. The word got out fast. I realized how secretive I had been about my illness. Now coaches, ex-players from multiple schools, neighbors, and friends were inquiring about my condition and praying for a quick recovery and for me to kick cancer's ass. The last part of that mostly came from my ex-players.

Then, at 8:00 a.m. on the nose, the media started calling to check on my status and attempting to line me up for interviews. It was nuts; I was getting calls statewide. I figured out later that it spread like wildfire because the guy who runs our team social media accounts tweeted my condition and plans for recovery late Friday night. Now the local media, including the Commercial Appeal and three local TV stations, wanted the story. My announcement had gone statewide in a matter of hours. As I sat at my kitchen table, the barrage of texts and calls were coming my way.

A high school beat reporter from Knoxville wanted the latest scoop. "Why Houston?"

"Why MD Anderson?"

"What kind of cancer?"

"Will you coach next season?"

"Are you terminal?"

"Now damn, that's a bold question," I snapped back. "No, I'm *not* terminal, and, yes, I will be at the helm next year. Got more work to do."

I hung up the phone.

By 9:30 a.m., tons of people were offering their prayers and condolences.

I was overwhelmed with the encouragement and motivation from everyone.

I made up my mind that I wanted to practice what I preached and keep distractions to a minimum in order to prepare for an incredible Arlington team that was also competing for home-field advantage going into round one of the playoffs. The winner was granted just that. But now, a ton of work needed to get going with game prep and improving our team to take on a terrific Arlington high school for senior night.

On Monday, central office was hammered with interview requests, and I told them I needed to keep focused, especially through Wednesday to get our team prepared. So, most of the week, I kept my head down to prepare our guys to be ready for senior night. However, I needed to do a couple interviews to thank the community for the prayers and let everyone know that Beth and I planned to fight this tooth and nail. Along with it being senior night, it was Breast Cancer Awareness night also. That week, I let the players wear pink accessories to acknowledge Breast Cancer Awareness. Also, I had ordered pink coaches' shirts early that fall for Friday's game long before I realized that I had cancer also. That certainly hit home for me personally when I wore it to school that Friday.

As the game prep continued, I realized Arlington had the advantage with their four-year starting all-state senior QB. Defensively, the game plan was to create pressure from all angles and move him around the pocket in the hope of preventing him from picking apart our young secondary. Arlington was well coached, and they had a solid game plan, not to mention their players just didn't care for the Dragons of Collierville at all. Behind Houston, Arlington was our next biggest rival.

As the week went on, the practices were solid. We kept distractions at bay, and our kids appeared focused. This was totally what I needed. Football was an excellent distraction. By Wednesday after practice, I agreed for some media interviews to put a positive light on our football team and the Collierville community; however, I also wanted people to understand my position in battling this terrible disease. I was going to hit this head on and just refuse to back down. Matter of fact, Saturday morning, after I went public with my diagnosis, I had Beth post on her Facebook Tom Petty's live concert rendition of "I Won't Back Down." She was glad to do this for me because she was getting so many questions and inquiries. At that time, I did very little social media outside of Snapchat with my own kids, and I never had a Facebook account. However, this blew up Beth's Facebook and was reposted on Twitter and Instagram as well. Eventually, a T-shirt fundraiser was done by the booster club and Kroger grocery store in Collierville. The shirts said, "Dragons Don't Back Down," and over 2,000 of them were sold to help with my travel expenses.

By Thursday, local news outlets continued to do stories about this being my last game to coach before I took off to Houston, Texas. On Friday, I agreed to do an in-depth interview with the biggest TV station in our region. I agreed to do it before the players arrived at the locker rooms to cut down on distractions. I did want to thank everyone for their kind thoughts and prayers and brag on the City of Collierville and surrounding communities for the support.

The station set it up in the field house for a one-on-one interview. In my pink Breast Cancer Awareness coach shirt, I answered questions about my plan for attacking this terrible foe. It was the first time in days my mind went back to cancer; however, it was important to get my message out.

Again, another exhausting week ended with a marathon day on Friday. I was tired. The cancer continued to grow in my tonsil, and I started to feel pain under my tongue. Furthermore, my lymph node in my neck was swollen to the size of a walnut, and I knew it was time to get my butt to Texas!

Everything that week was focused on football and school preparation. Right after the game, my focus would turn to Houston and the battle with cancer would begin. There would be no post-game film and no looking at next week's opponent. I promised that to myself, and I promised that to Beth. My energy and focus needed to shift to the transition to Texas.

At the same time, Beth was behind the scenes dealing with where dogs would stay, packing, and making travel and apartment arrangements. Our plan was to tie up any loose ends on Saturday and leave early Sunday morning to move into our new apartment that we leased for five months. Beth shielded me from that, and I cannot thank her enough. Once again, she allowed me to deal with the business of head coach, but she was right in the middle of us preparing to transfer to Houston, not to mention maintaining her high-demanding job. Our life was about to turn upside down for the foreseeable future.

Friday provided another unexpected challenge that, quite frankly, caught me off guard. Rain! Lots of rain. All week, there was only a 10 percent chance of scattered thunderstorms for Friday night. Damn, somehow that small system hit Collierville dead on the night we played Arlington. It started at pregame and continued to rain until almost the end of the fourth quarter.

When the game kicked off, I looked down and saw so many ex-Collierville/ CBHS players in the player box on the sideline. I loved to have ex-players hit the sidelines. Over the years, sometimes that can backfire with a penalty or two due to heckling of referees; however, overall, it's beneficial.

Tonight, this was a great showing for ex-players, even though it was pouring down rain. The crowd itself was average because of the weather, but overall, solid support was shown for the football program.

However, it was not a great night for the Dragons. Out of the gate, Arlington ran an unbalanced set to their sidelines in the form of a jet sweep that went eighty yards for their first score. It was 7-0 with eleven minutes left in the first quarter—not a good start. After going three and out on our first two drives, we began to settle down on defense and began working the game plan with the attempt to pressure and disrupt the passing game. That game plan was clearly not working. Our defensive linemen could not get any footing on the wet grass, and our blitzes were clearly hesitant due to lack of traction. Their QB and receivers ate our lunch. It was a dry field in the minds of Arlington, and the big plays murdered us. After we got on our heels and back in the zone coverage, they picked us apart. Our offense didn't have a chance to get into the game because of the big plays and field position we gave up all night. I was clearly outcoached, and we had zero plans in the event of a wet field. As a result, we were blown out 40-21 on a cold and rainy night.

As the game was deep in the fourth, I was pretty wiped out from the events over the past couple weeks. As the rain let up, I noticed the Collierville faithful had seen enough, but my family, friends, and pep clubs surrounded me as the first whistle was blown. At that time, Principal Blanchard and our booster club president, Scott Hendricks, had everyone in attendance surround me in the middle of the field. Also, the Arlington Tigers, headed by my friend, Coach Adam Sykes, presented me with a very nice VISA card to aid me in my journey. Right then, both teams joined one another for a prayer.

When they departed the field for the team bus back to Arlington, the administration, the booster club, and the pom and cheer teams presented me with memorabilia and further financial assistance that was quite simply overwhelming.

After the loss, I told the boys there was more work, and my responsibility was now handed over to interim head coach, Tommy Miller, and the football staff.

That night was extremely emotional for many, and I could tell Beth was feeling the effects of the last couple weeks. She looked worn out and visibly upset as we stood in the middle of the soggy, cold field surrounded by the Collierville faithful. I put my arm around her as she cried uncontrollably. It was a pure release of emotion that had been bottled up as she was in attack mode during the past two weeks in preparing for our battle against cancer.

As the night ended, family and close friends hung around until everyone departed.

"You guys have this. We are with you all the way," a neighbor firmly reminded us in an uplifting voice.

I looked at Beth with tears in her eyes, and I leaned over and reminded her, "We got this, honey."

Then, she looked me straight in my eye, cleared her throat, and said, "You're damn right we do!"

That night was the best sleep we both had in quite some time.

CHAPTER 32

TRICK OR TREAT

I WAS EXHAUSTED THAT Friday night after the Arlington game. The emotion, the transformation from head football coach to now cancer patient, and anticipated new resident in Houston, Texas, was staring me right in the face. Saturday was almost like a decompression day. It was like after the conclusion of every football season, the body and mind attempt to throttle down to a normal level. This year was obviously different in that the boys and coaching staff had more work to do. However, I completely stepped out of that mindset to focus on the transition to Houston and fighting cancer with every ounce of my being. I was able to do just that. Mentally, I redirected my thoughts and energy to the next challenge without any regrets.

That was a good thing because there wasn't any time to waste. Beth had packed and prepared almost everything for the transition, but there were still bits and pieces that needed to be tied up before our departure. We went to mass that Saturday evening, and I was anointed for last rights with a special blessing by our priest.

Next up was the eleven-hour trip to Houston, Texas. We were

locked and loaded; and the plan was to leave mid-Sunday morning and stop halfway in Texarkana, spend the night, and finish our trip to Houston to arrive early enough to unpack and set up our new apartment by Monday night.

As we left on Sunday, our neighbors, players, friends, and the community of Collierville offered me prayers and wished me safe travels. All day Sunday, I received phone calls and text messages from ex-players, friends, and colleagues to pass on words of encouragement. The players had the recurring theme of "Freakin' embrace it, coach! You've got this!"

One can read so many different things on the internet and that can be darn right dangerous. Beth researched constantly on the trip down. She is such a planner, organizer, and wanted to find any advantages we can to be successful in this battle while, at the same time, making our living arrangements as comfortable as possible.

As I was able to take off work, Beth was still working and needed to set up an office to be able to get some things accomplished while in our new apartment. After she set up the command center, she was investigating every option or obstacle that could possibly be thrown our way. My attitude was to stay off the internet and trust that I was in the best place in the world for cancer treatment. My angle was to be the best patient possible and have an incredible attitude no matter what direction my condition traveled. I also understood that I have lived an extremely blessed life with my soulmate, three incredible children, and two beautiful granddaughters. Also, I was loved and supported by my parents and siblings. Over the past twenty-eight years, I had lived my dream of coaching and working with kids. I knew that I was not ready to cash it in, but I also knew if my news was dire, my mind would be in a good place.

As we settled into our new surroundings in Houston's medical district that Monday, we went out to a nice dinner at nearby Rice Village. I knew when Tuesday morning arrived, it was go time. I was right. On October 31, I had multiple appointments out of the gate.

MDA likes to perform their own extensive tests. Any test that I had prior to showing up in Houston on that Halloween, MDA reevaluated and then some.

On day one, I was able to get familiar with my team of doctors. These professionals would perform evaluations through physicals, blood work, and scans. Some of these steps were extremely repetitive, but MDA does not leave any stone unturned.

After about my fifteenth nasal scope, MRI, PET scan, and CT scan, along with having my blood drawn, it was time for the tumor counsel of about seventy doctors and surgeons to look over my specific case and discuss a protocol.

I distinctly remember my visit with my doctor that Wednesday. My radiation oncologist brought in six colleagues (not students) to evaluate me individually. On six separate occasions, each doctor stuck their fingers down the back of my throat to physically determine where my tumor was located and the exact size of it. While this was happening, each doctor was writing frantically on a legal pad to document what they just evaluated. Almost like a team of coaches going to a future opponent football game to scout in person. I wasn't scared or intimidated whatsoever. I just knew this was part of the evaluation, so I thought about the advice I received from my players: "Freakin' embrace it!"

Back on the ninth floor, my lead doctor and surgeon explored the possibility of surgery. As he entered the room, I immediately felt at ease. He was extremely professional with an excellent bedside manner.

"Mr. O'Neill," he explained softly, "in evaluating your reports and scans, hopefully my services as a surgeon will not be needed. The tumor counsel will ultimately make that decision."

"What do you mean by that, sir?"

"There is an excellent chance we hit these tumors with radiation and chemo without surgery. If I were to remove them, you would get radiation and chemo additionally with the hope of destroying every cancer cell in your body. With the radiation and chemo method alone, there is roughly an 85 percent chance we put these tumors in remission without the scalpel."

I looked at Beth and witnessed a sigh of relief and thought, *That is welcome news.*

"Mike, the treatment I just mentioned is no walk in the park. However, with your age and physical makeup, you should respond to this procedure well."

My next appointment was with my internal oncologist, whose primary job was to recommend and explain my potential chemotherapy treatments. His office was also very detailed with physical examinations and blood work analysis to help determine the right treatment moving forward. Throughout the process, everything I experienced that first week was directed toward the meeting at the tumor council that happened every Thursday afternoon. Hopefully, by Friday, I would receive my treatment plan. Mentally and physically, I was ready to rock-n-roll.

Over the next four days, I had a total of twenty-one doctor's appointments to determine my cancer diagnosis and how to treat it. Friday morning, I was notified my treatment plan included thirty-three rounds of proton radiation with twelve weeks of chemotherapy lasting until late February.

That Friday I was appointment-free and turned my mind 100 percent toward the Collierville Dragons. Tonight's game would feature #2 seed Whitehaven and #6 seed Collierville in round one of Tennessee's State High School playoffs. Scott Hendrix would text and update me as the game unfolded. Between the Collierville football Twitter account and our booster club president reports, the information was flowing.

In the meantime, I wanted to get my football mindset on, so I convinced Beth and Mary to go check out some Texas high school football. I hadn't been to a game in Texas since watching my younger brother Parks play for Lake Highlands High School in the Dallas area when my parents moved back to Texas in the late '80s. Now I was jonesing to check out powerhouse Katy High School play at their new $70 million high school football stadium, which was about forty-five minutes due west of Houston. At 7:00 p.m. sharp, I was anticipating the Dragons and Tigers matchup back in Memphis.

Beth, Mary, and I arrived early to take in the sights and pageantry leading up to a Texas high school football game. Nowhere else in the U.S. can you get this from a high school sport, but on a fall Friday night in Texas. We arrived with plenty of time and parked ourselves on the forty-yard line on the home side of this magnificent high school stadium.

As I took a bite of some brisket BBQ nachos, I received a phone call from our athletic director from the playoff game at Whitehaven.

"Both teams are back in the locker room due to lightning in the south Memphis area. The teams went out for pregame and then boom."

The rule in Tennessee was that the contest would be delayed a minimum of thirty minutes after the last strike of lightning in the surrounding area. The AD then added that our guys were now back in a small, cramped Whitehaven locker room, which would eventually last an hour.

"Our guys look focused and ready to play. I have a good feeling about this," he stated.

Back in Texas, it was clear and seventy-two degrees as we witnessed Katy dispense a beatdown on their week ten opponent. The playoffs in Texas would start the following week. As the Collierville game was delayed, I was able to experience the Texas high school football atmosphere and quickly noticed the sheer size of Katy's football team: massive. *Dang,* I thought, *everything* is *bigger in Texas, at least at Katy High School.*

In West Tennessee, the Collierville Dragons had a chance to shock the state with a huge upset by playing the angle of winning one for the coach. Tonight, they would need that help because when the rain delay was over, they would play a football team with no less than six Division I athletes and would furthermore send a total of twenty players to continue at the collegiate level. The Tiger offensive linemen were not as big as Katy's, but they were giants compared to us and clocked in around 300 pounds up front compared to our 240-pound guys in the trenches. Furthermore, Whitehaven's team speed was ridiculous. Overall, we had two advantages: the kicking game and our three-year starting QB, Matt Connors. However, one thing that does not show up in the stats sheet is heart!

The game started fast! Both teams scored on their first drives. The Dragons then scored on their second drive, and the defense began to frustrate Whitehaven when our guys were flying around the ball. I was pretty much on the phone with Scott Hendrix all game. Collierville took the halftime lead. The second half was also a back-and-forth contest. Unfortunately, late in the fourth, Whitehaven was able to get their prolific power offense on track, and the Dragons came up short with the potential game-winning drive stalling at the Tiger twenty-five-yard line.

As Whitehaven took a knee in victory formation, I couldn't be any prouder of the heart and effort displayed that November night by our football team. After the game, I put together a group text to our guys to express just how proud I was of them. Later, I learned they had a great week of practice and were extremely focused. Coach Miller and the staff did an excellent job of getting our guys ready to play, and I couldn't thank them enough for their efforts. Coach Rodney Saulsberry, the head coach at Whitehaven, was quoted in the Commercial Appeal newspaper as saying: "I was worried all week because I knew the Collierville football team would show up ready to play on behalf of Coach O'Neill." That really touched my heart because he was spot on. The Dragons played their asses off for four quarters and never quit.

Later around midnight, the game film was uploaded, and I went through the game play by play. My head hit the pillow around 3:30 a.m. It felt like my typical Friday night back in the 901.

CHAPTER 33

NEW BEGINNING, TOUGH ENDING

B Y MARCH 2018, we were packing up the apartment to move back to Tennessee. The last four months were certainly not easy with the treatment plan I was required to follow.

One of the biggest challenges was to avoid the feeding tube by maintaining sufficient caloric intake. Food in my view was essentially medicine. The numerous rounds of radiation destroyed all my taste-buds and burnt my throat inside and out. Eating was the last thing on my mind, so the task of consuming every bite was daunting. Ulti-mately, I lost forty pounds before my weight stabilized.

The daily radiation and weekly chemotherapy tested my faith and mental stability every single time I went to the proton center or chemo ward. Being strapped down on a cold table with a custom-made fiber-glass hockey mask accompanied with a protective mouthpiece while not moving one millimeter for sixty minutes thirty-three times is zero fun; however, I realized every session I completed, I was one step closer in winning my battle against cancer. Every day I came home from the proton center, I would gladly mark through the calendar on the refrigerator until I achieved my goal. A great attitude was paramount during that time.

Through all those difficult times, I must say there was plenty of silver lining. First, Beth and I were able to spend quality time together in our extremely busy lives. The small apartment, walking distance from the hospital, was ideal and provided generous time in each other's presence to endure the intensity of our circumstances. Basically, we took a break from our fast-paced lives. We both agreed that our time together was an immense blessing.

Mary was able to join us during our time in Houston. She had recently graduated college and wanted to help in any way she could. During that time, she rediscovered her talent as a vocalist and was able to work with a renown vocal coach in the Houston area who took her talent to another level. In those four months, she ran endless errands, provided needed comic relief, and was able to begin her music career that continues to this day.

Brooke and my granddaughter Mary Reagan spent some valuable time with us at the height of the treatment. Their presence provided much needed love, happiness, and encouragement during that difficult time, which accelerated my recovery. Their timing was perfect.

Michael planned a trip in the early days of treatment to organize the purchase of an engagement ring, and also to plot a well-timed beautiful setting to ask his unassuming longtime girlfriend Christi for her hand in marriage in the heart of Houston.

Those four months in Texas brought so many wonderful memories during a very grueling time in our lives. There is very little doubt, these uplifting times provided the strength and perseverance to tolerate this unexpected brutal treatment.

By the time we returned to Shelby County, I rejoined the Collierville team for off-season weight workouts in late March and was back in the classroom in early April. My first day back was incredible and everyone was so nice. During first period, the Collierville fight song was performed by members of the band to welcome me back to school. Banners were displayed around the school, with colleagues and students dropping by all day long. I can't thank everyone enough for the generosity and prayers said on my behalf. Also, I'm grateful to Principal Blanchard and the rest of the Collierville teachers and administrators for their kind gestures and messages throughout my cancer journey.

From a professional perspective, my days in Houston were somewhat productive at least from a football position. Before the thirty-three rounds of radiation took place, I was able to go to several Katy High

School games and attended a handful of practices to get a feel for how a top-notch program in Texas handles the business of high school football.

Upon my return, the athletic facilities at Collierville High School were now in full construction mode after the football stadium and turf room had broken ground in January. Superintendent John Aitken and Principal Chip Blanchard insisted on providing a full tour for the new school and football facility. They were desperately trying to make the first game deadline in August for the 2018 season opener.

On a very chilly late March afternoon, I pulled in the future Collierville High School parking lot to meet the superintendent and principal for a guided tour.

"Coach, let's walk through the school, and then we will get to the fun stuff," Mr. A said in his famous Tennessee southern drawl.

We spent the next forty-five minutes covering the grounds of the education wing of the new school. This would be one of the largest public high schools in Tennessee, and every department and head coach had their hand in during the planning stage two years prior. Some plans were approved; some were not. But it was massive.

As we completed the tour of the main school building, we then exited the school's basketball coliseum to head across the grounds to the football facility. I couldn't help myself; I was smiling from ear to ear.

"Mike," Chip asked, "what do you think about this field house entrance?"

I was almost speechless. I thought, *I can't believe everyone approved this building. To my knowledge, there is not another one like it in West Tennessee, and at some point, it will be a game changer for attracting athletes. Thanks for pushing for it, Mr. A.*

The tour continued into the football stadium that included field turf, opposing press boxes, and a jumbotron. The locker room and coaches' offices were state of the art.

"You guys didn't hold anything back, did you? I can see almost everything was approved," I said.

"We told you to shoot for the moon, O'Neill, and hopefully we responded," Mr. A said.

"Y'all sure did. Thank you!" I cheerfully said.

"There is a ton of construction left, and if the weather cooperates, we should be ready for the season opener, according to the construction super," Chip added.

Upon returning to the weight room, I was at it again and getting ready for spring practice at the end of May. The players made solid gains under Coach Miller, and before I knew it, we were in the summer grind to build up to the 2018 season. This year would be a bit different with the transition to the new stadium and facilities.

During the 2018 preseason, I started to develop severe headaches. At that time, I was committed to the grind of the season and tried to play it off. Furthermore, I felt guilty for leaving my team and staff right before the playoffs and an additional five months in the off-season. I couldn't waste one second. The combination of preparing an inexperienced and relatively young team for a very hard schedule, updating equipment, and preparing the transition from the old stadium, weight room, and other equipment, only intensified my condition.

As the buildup to the season was underway, our young team was focused on Mississippi State powerhouse Olive Branch for game one. They lost the state championship the previous season and had only lost one game for the entire year. So, we prepped most of the summer for them. It was critical that we win our first game in the new stadium.

Our kids worked their tails off thinking that the 2018 season opener would be played at our new stadium; however, we were informed we would open at Herman Osteen (the old stadium) due to construction delays from spring rains. Our guys wouldn't miss a beat, even though we had our work cut out for us. With four brand-new linebackers, a new starting QB, and four sophomore offensive starting linemen, the guys played with passion. We were tied going into the fourth, but eventually lost by a touchdown in a low-scoring game. That summer we employed a Tampa-two defense that gave Olive Branch fits, keeping their offense out of rhythm the entire game. We just came up short on the offensive side with only three returning starters. I was proud of their effort.

After winning the next two, our stadium date was pushed out to yet another possible opening of the stadium. Pressure mounted for us. We lost our last game at the old stadium and two of my assistant coaches received personal foul calls that resulted in me being kicked out of the contest with less than two minutes remaining in the game.

This was a boiling point. I had never been so disappointed! Not only because it was the last game at Herman Osteen Field; the overall punishment would carry over for an additional game (when we were to open the new stadium), according to the referee who threw the second flag. As I was heading off the sidelines to leave the game, my mind was overwhelmed with everything that just happened. That last game at the old stadium was certainly forgettable to say the least and the headaches only continued to intensify.

The next morning, I spoke with the athletic director and principal, and we decided to contest the decision made by the referee on Friday night. It was decided to appeal the decision after talking to the director of officials because he indicated under the current rules, I shouldn't have been ejected to begin with, much less suspended for another week. That morning we completed the paperwork for the Tennessee Secondary School Athletic Association to appeal the decision about me coaching on Friday night. By Wednesday, the TSSAA ruled on my behalf, and I was able to join the team for the first game in the new stadium. This was a huge relief!

That week, we put our heads down and prepped for Wooddale for the grand opening of the new stadium. In the meantime, the sharp pains in my forehead and the back of my neck only continued. I was informed by MD Anderson to reach out to a neurologist in Memphis for a CAT scan, and it was determined that it was caused by my thirty-three rounds of radiation, and I needed time to recover from my treatment. I will say I was warned by my doctors at MD Anderson that I was returning too soon, and I would feel the repercussions if I wasn't careful.

The Wooddale week was solid, and we won in a decisive way; however, I gave up the defensive coordination job because of my condition. Sadly, I got to the point where I couldn't project my voice and my stamina started to suffer. I was extremely frustrated, but I knew I needed more time to recover from my treatment.

The Wooddale game was great for the program and was special to me as well. My mom was able to see me coach one more time before passing away that next spring, and Mary Elizabeth sang the national anthem to perfection before an outstanding crowd to open our new stadium. It was a perfect night with a score of 42 – 0.

As the season continued, we were 5-5 heading into the playoffs, and the youth of our offensive line was starting to rear its ugly head. Injuries were mounting and we had sophomores replacing sophomores; they were being thrown into the fire. Our guys never gave up and continued to work every day. And yes, game one of the playoffs was back to southwest Memphis to play an excellent Whitehaven High School team. We were blown out.

After the season came to an abrupt stop, I started to think about my immediate future in high school football. Beth and I would spend the next three weeks talking about the past couple years and my continued recovery moving forward. With a combination of prayer and soul-searching, I concluded I needed time away from the strenuous demands of running the high school football program to recover from the taxing cancer treatments from earlier in the year. It would be one of the most heart-wrenching decisions I had ever made in life.

The Monday after the football banquet, I shot Mr. Blanchard an email during first period to set up a time to meet after my last class had concluded.

At 12:15 p.m. sharp, I sat outside Chip's closed office when it abruptly opened, and a downcast student walked out.

"Come in, coach. Sorry for the wait," he said, shaking his head in mild disgust from the prior meeting.

"Thanks for seeing me on such short notice," I said as we shook hands.

"Have a seat, Mike," he said as he closed the door of his office.

My heart rate jumped slightly as I sat in the comfortable leather chair directly across from him.

"Chip, I need to talk to you about my coaching future, but I wanted to wait until the conclusion of the football banquet to avoid any distractions for the outgoing season."

"Okay, coach. You have my attention. What's on your mind?"

"This isn't going to be easy for me to say. Through several hours of soul-searching, reflection, and conversations with my wife, I have made a tough decision to step down from my post as head coach for the football program. I need time to recover from my treatments, and I refuse to hold the program hostage another second in order to do that."

I went on to explain in full detail of the months of reoccurring headaches and other limitations that were derailing my ability to coach at the optimal level.

"Chip, I need to step down and take care of my health because I have ignored it simply too long, and it almost killed me last year," I said as a tear began to surface.

"Coach, stop. I get it. I didn't mean to interrupt you, but we, the administration, were all somewhat surprised you were able to pick up as soon as you did. Your health and your family have been through a ton, and I will certainly respect any decision you make. It sounds like you did just that," he said in a compassionate voice.

"Yes, sir," I said while I gazed at the carpet. "I have made that decision, and maybe down the road, I can catch up with the new staff at some opportunity."

"Coach O'Neill, you take as long as you need to concentrate on your recovery. You can teach at Collierville as long as you like. I'm a bit surprised, but I totally get it. You will be sorely missed on the field, and you have done a great job in rebuilding the program. Thank you."

I felt a sense of relief and appreciated Chip's response. I also felt his compassion and willingness to listen to my dilemma. Superintendent John Aitken was extremely caring and supportive of my decision also. I asked Chip if I could inform the coaches and players before we broke for Christmas.

He replied, "Absolutely."

That afternoon, I had the office make an announcement for all returning players and coaches to attend a mandatory meeting in the field house—now cleared for occupancy—that day. I always wanted to do something as a head coach in the building that I worked tirelessly for. Unfortunately, this wasn't exactly what I had in mind.

As I walked into the entrance, I was almost overcome with a mixture of elation and sadness. When asked three years ago, "What is on the top of your list?" This was absolutely it. Now, I was surrounded by eighty players and coaches to inform them that I needed to step away from the game and team that I loved very much. It was one of the hardest things I'd ever done in my life. But I knew my health and recovery demanded it. For too long, I had put my health on the backburner, and now was the time that I needed to put that on the top of my priority list.

While I waited for the remaining underclassmen to gather in the middle of the turf room, I invited the players to have a seat. I cleared my voice.

"Men, thank you for making this meeting on short notice. Coaches, I promise not to be long so everyone can start their Christmas break as soon as possible. If we are missing anyone, please pass on this message.

"Gentlemen, this will not be easy for me, but I will get right to the point. I'm stepping down as head football coach to focus on my cancer treatment and recovery."

The players in the back, having private conversations, shifted their attention in my direction.

"With a ton of discussion with my wife, family, and doctors, I need to do this, men. Coaches, I apologize for not providing you with ample warning, but I just informed Principal Blanchard about this decision. Both of our athletic directors are at a conference in Texas. They don't even know. I just wanted to make this announcement before the break and provide ample time for the administration to find your next coach. I was not going to drag this out any longer than necessary." I closed my eyes for a moment.

"Guys, as I step down and take some time away from football, you need to understand your time is *now*. Look around you. You have everything at your disposal. You have a new stadium, weight room, locker room, and this incredible fifty-yard indoor turf room. There is absolutely no reason, in a short amount of time, you can't compete for a state championship. Men, that is why you play this game: to compete at the highest level possible. A state championship needs to be your goal every year from here on out. You watch—players will come out of the woodwork to be part of this program because they see the opportunity and potential it has. Kids that play other sports here at Collierville will start playing football. You watch. Players from other schools or out of town will move to Collierville over time with the sole purpose of going to this great high school and using these facilities. You'll see, some of your buddies going to private schools will transfer back to the 'Ville to be a part of this program. Build it, and they will come. You've heard of that saying, right? You watch; great things are about to happen here."

I took a deep breath and took a pull from my water bottle.

"No, I don't have a clue who the next head coach will be. He might be in this room now; he might be in another state. But what I can tell you, men, no matter who it is, you will need to give it up for him on day one in order to get this program to the next level! I didn't work my tail off at Collierville over the last decade to see this program take one step back. No, sir. Do not settle for that. I'll be watching you, and I'm excited for your future. I'm still a Dragon, and I will continue to teach here… One last thing, gentlemen: Thanks for the opportunity to coach you. And coaches, thank you for all your help. Go Dragons, and Merry Christmas!"

As I spoke to them about their future and growing this program into a state contender, I couldn't help but reflect on how the program was near rock bottom when I took over as the interim coach and how this program was now moving in the right direction. Yes, I didn't win a coveted gold ball—not even close. However, I truly believed I put every ounce of zeal that I could every time I put on that whistle… In not cutting corners, working hard, and playing by the rules, I could sleep at night and be proud of our guys. Collectively, we weren't blessed with a tremendous amount of speed and size, but our guys brought their lunch box most every day and flat out got after it.

As the meeting broke with hugs and well wishes, I could sense a bit of relief. I knew it was the time to get my health back on track and spend some much needed time with my wife and family. Life was way too short not to.

As I pulled out of the football complex, I was proud to see the new stadium, locker room, and field house come together. Furthermore, I looked over and saw the massive dragon on the fifty-yard line; I was glad the powers that be kept that incredible dragon mascot design the football team began using on their helmets some six years ago during my tenure. I anticipated seeing it every time I passed the school on 385. I believed Collierville football would be a state contender in the not-so-distant future.

CHAPTER 34

ONE YEAR LATER

"OKAY, GIRLS, PILE in," I gently advised as we loaded up the truck to hit 40 East.

"Where are we going, G-Daddy?" my granddaughter Mary Reagan curiously asked.

"We are going to an awesome waterpark in Nashville. Who's ready?" I yelled the question as two giant smiles, including my youngest granddaughter Palmer's, radiating from the backseat.

The past summer Beth and I decided to introduce the first annual weeklong Lala & G-daddy camp to spend quality time with our grand girls. Next September, our first grandson Andrew Michael will join the party and we plan to keep the tradition going.

Life can change on a dime. Two summers ago, I was running youth football camps, while preparing the varsity team for the upcoming fall season.

One year later, my life has changed in so many ways. First, in May 2021, I officially retired from Collierville schools to focus on my cancer battle. In addition, since my cancer metastasized in both lungs, the multiple tumors have increased in size but not at an alarming rate. I currently fly to MD Anderson every three weeks to take part in an immunotherapy trial specific to my cancer with the hope my immune system will recognize cancer cells in my body and destroy them. While the tumors have grown about 20 percent since the trial began, no new lesions have formed. My doctor informed me that thirty years ago I might not be so lucky. Something positive is happening, and hopefully future trials will perhaps knock it out completely one day. Currently, I'm plugged into three excellent cancer centers and continue to seek the latest treatment on the horizon.

My attitude continues to remain positive, and my side effects from the trial meds are minimal, outside of periodic periods of fatigue with random minor digestive issues. One thing I have surmised while fighting cancer, a *positive attitude* is more than half the battle.

During the past year of reflection, I now understand miscalculations in my youth and early adulthood which resulted in steady growth from those setbacks. Quitting football my junior year provided a unique opportunity to coach my kid brother's youth football team, which would set off a chain of events that would impact me moving forward. Making a comeback my senior year resulted in several of the most powerful life lessons I would never forget:

Anything is Possible

The time spent with some incredible mentors and teammates in winning a state championship and having the opportunity to coach before my playing career was over is a feat you rarely witness. That process allowed me to experience an incredible senior football season through the lens of a coach and that experience is what kindled my love for coaching. After that, I was officially bit by the coaching bug, and it created my desire to pursue my lifelong passion. At times, I pretended my drive to teach and coach wasn't there and I needed to pursue a business career to obtain a better lifestyle. However, in those times of adversity and setback, I came to realize my true dream and eventually embraced it with the encouragement of my soulmate. For that reason, I have no regrets.

Adversity

There is absolutely no way around this one. Life will dish it out. For me, it came in the form of injuries, facing reality as a young adult, and numerous life-altering events that at times were self-induced. It wasn't until I met Beth that I really started to understand the true meaning of adversity and how to advance through it. The summer and fall of '89 provided an ample supply of roadblocks to our love story and how we approached it. For a prolonged period, it seemed we dealt with endless issues, which truly created an everlasting bond in our relationship. In short, work the problem, whatever it may be. Learn from failure, adapt, and move on. Do not let the issue mutate before any action is taken. These early lessons as a young couple helped us prepare for our biggest test: facing an unexpected cancer diagnosis that came some thirty years later. Backing down is not an option.

Opportunity

When one door closes, look for one to open, even if you must kick it down. My junior year provided so many opportunities after I began coaching. The year I left Christian Brothers provided an incredible opportunity right in my backyard.

Keep an open heart to learn what your spiritual gifts may be, then seize the opportunity when they are presented. Once you figure out your true passion, understand the path needed to pursue and obtain it.

Opportunity is all around us, however, it's not always entirely obvious.

Silver Lining

In life, negative events are bound to happen. It's very easy to be consumed by misery or anguish because of the obvious setback or pain. Always look for the silver lining when life throws you a curveball.

My terrible news of being diagnosed with throat cancer in 2017, right when life was as busy as ever, created an environment in which we were forced to slow down and deal with my dire situation. That valuable time spent together with Beth only expanded our bond and love for one another. One must look for some positive context in any misfortune.

Power of Prayer

I will say that life goes on. Our family is no different from many others; we have encouraged our kids to continue living heathy and productive lives and to seek out their own benevolent path. Continue to be open and flexible when life is tough and don't forget the power of daily prayer.

Personally, I've witnessed the power of prayer through the miracle of Novenas, being motivated to convert to Catholicism by the Holy Spirit and receiving God's guiding light during my fierce battle with cancer. Honestly, I cannot understand how people exist without talking to God on a regular basis.

Beth continues to be the rock in our family—her encouragement, faith, and relentless love have been there from the start. I'm so blessed our paths crossed and we continue to share a beautiful life and family together.

She reminds me from time to time that her grandfather, H.B. Clark, gave us that special blessing on our wedding day. He prayed, "I ask God to bless you both with a long, happy life and endless happiness between you."

From June 11, 2020, through June 11, 2021, I learned so much about myself by reflecting on life's events. It provided an incredible, unique opportunity to self-reflect about life and how decisions, both good and bad, can alter life instantaneously or perhaps years later.

The overall purpose of writing my story was for my family, future grandchildren, and generations to come. At the time I started, I simply didn't know how much time I have left.

One thing is for sure: nothing is guaranteed in this world, so never take anything for granted. My faith, my attitude, and the ability to have an open heart for life's incredible gifts has made my journey meaningful and beautiful.

I'm beyond blessed and can't thank God enough that He has given me the wisdom to pursue my special gifts without any regrets. I also thank God in granting me an open heart to find my *forever* soulmate.

The End

ACKNOWLEDGEMENTS

After learning in March of 2020 that my cancer had returned, my wife and father encouraged me to write a book. On separate occasions, they encouraged me to tell my story. Unsure of how long I might have with my family, I was inspired to leave a legacy for my children, grandchildren, and future generations. So, I began journaling, and the book project was born on June 11, 2020. I wrote for one year putting the pen down on June 11, 2021. My handwritten manuscript exceeded 160,000 words. *My keyboarding skills are average at best.* I spent 4-6 hours each day writing the first and second draft by hand. My research told me to write fast, edit slow. After the fast write portion, I realized I needed to clean it up. My handwriting is atrocious, and by month eleven, my forearm and shoulder were about to fall off. This is when the fun part started.

My wife shared the news *that I had finished handwriting the book* on her CaringBridge journal - with her *warranted* concern as to how we would translate my awful handwriting into a digital form. The post generated a team of volunteers. I copied the notebooks and separated them by chapter. To this team…thank you. Beth O'Neill, Brooke Clement, Mary Elizabeth O'Neill, Christi Picus O'Neill, Cassidy Beall, Dawn Mundy, Cherrie Reed, and Michaela Lott. I can't thank you all enough! This was a true labor of love.

Special thanks to Dawn Mundy, a retired certified medical transcriber, neighbor, and friend, who volunteered to type the last 12 chapters and simply turned into the offensive coordinator of the book project. She organized and formatted each chapter into the first digital draft of the project.

Sarah Fox, Founder and CEO of "The Bookish Fox", and her team did a fantastic job of working with me to translate the massive 160,000-word manuscript into a readable memoir format. Sarah encouraged me to "show more than tell" and inspired me to create more "scenes and dialog" throughout the book. Her team provided three incredible edits with invaluable feedback. Thank you!

My friend and high school football teammate, Dr. Marshall Boswell (Author/English Professor- Rhodes College), affirmed Sarah's feedback. Marshall helped me understand that it's okay to let the details go for the recommended shortened memoir version. I will always have the original manuscript for my family.

My research led me to Damon Freeman, Founder and Creative Director of "Damonza". Damon designed the book cover creating several phenomenal options to consider. I shared the options with hundreds of friends, family members, colleagues, former football players, and Collierville High School business teachers, Geraldine McBride and Matthew Kelley. Geraldine and Matthew created a marketing assignment requiring specific feedback and rankings from their high school students. The feedback from everyone helped me select the book cover you see today. Thanks to everyone for providing your input and ranking your favorite design. Damon, thanks for hitting it out of the park on the cover!

I'm grateful to all those who read chapters, helped me recall dates and facts, and provided feedback throughout my book journey. Thank you! Especially to my family who are the largest part of my life journey. My sincere appreciation to my soulmate, Beth, who completes me. My children, Brooke, Michael, and Mary Elizabeth who have always been the greatest joy of our life. My father, Ron O'Neill, for always encouraging me. My mother, Nancy O'Neill, who was the best mother and grandmother. I love you all dearly!

Tom Petty's song, *I Won't Back Down*, has been a source of

inspiration. I would listen to this song when feeling terrible during my cancer treatments. The 2017 Collierville football team turned this into "Don't Back Down" making signs and writing notes of encouragement. This became the constant "theme" for my journey and seemed to be the most appropriate title for the book. Thank you.

Last, but not least, I want to thank God for his numerous blessings, my faith, for providing me strength, good health, and the mental capability to collect and document my thoughts to complete this book for my family and generations to come. He is the source of all strength and everything good. Joshua 1:9

Ron O'Neill, Christi, Michael & baby Andrew O'Neill, Mike & Beth O'Neill, Mary O'Neill, Brooke, Bowers, Mary Reagan & Palmer Clement

AUTHOR BIO

Mike O'Neill is a first-time author with his debut memoir, *Don't Back Down.*

Following a decade in sales & marketing, the Tennessee native turned his attention to his true passion of mentoring youth through football coaching and teaching business and marketing classes. O'Neill coached middle school football for eight years before transitioning to high school football, first at Christian Brothers High then at Collierville High, where he spent the last seven years of his 20-year tenure as Head Football Coach. In 2017, O'Neill was named the Region 7-6A Coach of the Year.

Due to his first cancer diagnosis and search for treatment, O'Neill retired from coaching in 2018. That same year he was named the 2018 Collierville Man of the Year and was a Courage Thru Cancer honoree. He also received the Mario Reed Courage Award from the National Football Foundation and College Football Hall of Fame. Despite another stage 4 diagnosis in 2020, O'Neill brings his "A" game through his faith and determination to overcome adversity.

He graduated from the University of Memphis with a BA in Business Management and later pursued his MA in Education to commit to his dream of coaching.

O'Neill lives in Piperton, TN, with his beloved Beth and French bulldog Joey. When he's not chasing the latest cure for cancer, he enjoys traveling and spending time with family.

Milton Keynes UK
Ingram Content Group UK Ltd.
UKHW011125080124
435661UK00006B/612